BEASTIE BOYS

HIP-HOP STARS

Beastie Boys
Sean Combs
Missy Elliott
Eminem
Jay-Z
LL Cool J
Queen Latifah
Run-DMC
Tupac Shakur
Russell Simmons

HIP-HOP STARS

BEASTIE BOYS

Dennis Abrams

CHELSEA HOUSE
PUBLISHERS
An imprint of Infobase Publishing

BEASTIE BOYS

Chelsea House
An imprint of Infobase Publishing
132 West 31st Street
New York, NY 10001

Library of Congress Cataloging-in-Publication Data

Abrams, Dennis, 1960–
  Beastie Boys / Dennis Abrams.
     p. cm. — (Hip-hop stars)
  Includes bibliographical references (p.) and index.
  Discography: p.
  ISBN-13: 978-0-7910-9480-8 (hardcover)
  ISBN-10: 0-7910-9480-4 (hardcover)
  1. Beastie Boys—Juvenile literature. 2. Rap musicians—United States—Biography—Juvenile literature. I. Title. II. Series.

  ML3930.B38A63 2007
  782.42164092'2—dc22   2007000970
  [B]

Chelsea House books are available at special discounts when purchased in bulk quantities for businesses, associations, institutions, or sales promotions. Please call our Special Sales Department in New York at (212) 967-8800 or (800) 322-8755.

You can find Chelsea House on the World Wide Web at http://www.chelseahouse.com

Text design by Erik Lindstrom
Cover design by Ben Peterson

Printed in the United States of America

Bang NMSG 10 9 8 7 6 5 4 3 2 1

This book is printed on acid-free paper.

All links and Web addresses were checked and verified to be correct at the time of publication. Because of the dynamic nature of the Web, some addresses and links may have changed since publication and may no longer be valid.

CONTENTS

Hip-Hop: A Brief History

Like the air we breathe, hip-hop seems to be everywhere. The lifestyle that many thought would be a passing fad has, three decades later, grown to become a permanent part of world culture. Hip-hop artists have become some of today's heroes, replacing the comic book worship of decades past and joining athletes and movie stars as the people kids dream of being. Names like 50 Cent, P. Diddy, Russell Simmons, Jay-Z, Foxy Brown, Snoop Dogg, and Flavor Flav now ring as familiar as Elvis, Babe Ruth, Marilyn Monroe, and Charlie Chaplin.

While the general public knows many of the names, videos, and songs branded by the big companies that make them popular, it's also important to know the holy trinity, the founding fathers of hip-hop: Kool DJ Herc, Grandmaster Flash, and

Afrika Bambaataa. All are deejays who played and presented the records that rappers and dancers delighted themselves upon. Bambaataa single-handedly stopped the gang wars in the 1970s with the themes of peace, unity, love, and having fun.

Hip-hop is simply a term for a form of artistic creativity that was spawned in New York City—more precisely, the Bronx—in the early to mid-1970s. Amidst the urban decay in the areas where black and Hispanic people dwelled, economic, educational, and environmental resources were depleted. Jobs and businesses were all but moved away. Living conditions were of a lower standard than the rest of the city and country. Last but not least, art and sports programs in the schools were the first to be cut for the sake of lowering budgets; thus, music classes, teaching the subject's history and techniques, were all but lost.

From these ashes, like a phoenix, rose an art form. Through the love of technology and records found in family collections or even those tossed out on the street, the deejay emerged. Different from the ones heard on the radio, these folk were innovating a style that was popular on the island of Jamaica. Two turntables kept the music continuous, with the occasional voice on top of the records. This was the very humble beginning of rap music.

Rap music is actually two distinct words: rap and music. "Rap" is the vocal application that is used on top of the music. On a vocal spectrum, it is between talking and singing and is one of the few alternatives for vocalizing to emerge in the past 50 years. It's important to know that inventors and artists are side by side in the importance of music's development. Let's remember that inventor Thomas A. Edison created the first recording, with "Mary Had a Little Lamb" in 1878, most likely in New Jersey, the same state where the first rap recording— Sugarhill Gang's "Rapper's Delight"— was made more than 100 years later, in 1979.

It's hard to separate the importance of history, science, language arts, and education when discussing music. Because of the social silencing of black people in the United States from slavery in the 1600s to civil rights in the 1960s, much sentiment, dialogue, and soul is wrapped within the cultural expression of music. In eighteenth-century New Orleans, slaves gathered on Sundays in Congo Square to socialize and play music. Within this captivity many dialects, customs, and styles combined with instrumentation, vocals, and rhythm to form a musical signal or code of preservation. These are the foundations of jazz and the blues. Likewise, it's impossible to separate hip-hop and rap music from the creativity of the past. Look within the expression and words of black music and you'll get a reflection of history itself. The four creative elements of hip-hop—emcee-ing (the art of vocalization); deejaying (the musician-like manipulation of records); break dancing (the body expression of the music); and graffiti (the drawn graphic expression of the culture)—have been intertwined in the community before and since slavery.

However, just because these expressions were introduced by the black–Hispanic underclass, doesn't mean that others cannot create or appreciate hip-hop. Hip-hop is a cultural language used best to unite the human family all around the world. To peep the global explosion, one need not search far. Starting just north of the U.S. border, Canadian hip-hop has featured indigenous rappers who are infusing different language and dialect flows into their work, from Alaskan Eskimo to French flowing cats from Montreal and the rest of Quebec's provincial region. Few know that France for many years has been the second largest hip-hop nation, measured not just by high sales numbers, but also by a very political philosophy. Hip-hop has been alive and present since the mid-1980s in Japan and other Asian countries. Australia has been a hotbed in welcoming world rap acts, and it has also created its own vibrant hip-hop scene, with the reminder of its government's takeover of indigenous people reflected in every rapper's flow and rhyme. As a rhythm of the people, the continents of Africa and South America (especially Ghana, Senegal, and South Africa, Brazil, Surinam, and Argentina) have long mixed traditional homage into the new beats and rhyme of this millennium.

Hip-hop has been used to help Brazilian kids learn English when school systems failed to bridge the difficult language gap of Portuguese and patois to American English. It has entertained and enlightened youth, and has engaged political discussion in society, continuing the tradition of the African griots (storytellers) and folk singers.

For the past 25 years, hip-hop has been bought, sold, followed, loved, hated, praised, and blamed. History has shown that other cultural music forms in the United States have been just as misunderstood and held under public scrutiny. The history of the people who originated the art form can be found in the music itself. The timeline of recorded rap music spans more than a quarter century, and that is history in itself.

Presidents, kings, queens, fame, famine, infamy, from the great wall of China to the Berlin wall, food, drugs, cars, hate, and love have been rhymed and scratched. This gives plenty reason for social study. And I don't know what can be more fun than learning the history of something so relevant to young minds and souls, as music.

That's Not Who We Are

They are one of the most influential groups of our time. They were the first important white rap group. By combining rap with punk rock, they made rap music accessible to white kids. As leaders in sampling from a selection of wildly diverse and unexpected recordings, they have become the hipster's hip-hop group of choice. Two of their six albums made *Rolling Stone* magazine's list of "The 500 Greatest Albums of All Time." Their first album was the best-selling rap record of the 1980s. They have sold over 22 million records in the United States alone, surpassing such legendary artists as the Beach Boys and Stevie Wonder.

Critic Matt Diehl wrote in his *Rolling Stone* review of their album *Ill Communication*, "Since the Beasties earliest recordings ... their mission remains intact: to explore the unifying

One of the most influential hip-hop groups in music history, the Beastie Boys are *(left to right)* Adam Horovitz (Ad-Rock), Adam Yauch (MCA), and Mike Diamond (Mike D). The first popular white rap group, the Beastie Boys defied racial stereotypes and sold more than 22 million records nationwide. Mixing punk rock and rap, they are known for their unique sound and their experimental attitude towards music.

threads between hip-hop and punk, taking their basic elements—the scratch of a needle across a vinyl groove, a pounding snare-bass thump, the crunch of a power chord—and slicing them up with a Ginsu knife." They are considered a sure thing to be elected to the Rock and Roll Hall of Fame.

They are the Beastie Boys.

When the group first emerged on the music scene in the mid-1980s, none of the above statements would have seemed at all likely or even possible. Nobody would have ever dreamed of calling them "artists." They were seen as a novelty act whose popularity would quickly end. Their image was that of three macho clowns. They acted like drunk frat boys who had somehow managed to make a hit record. Their first album was *Licensed to Ill.* The hit single was "(You Gotta) Fight for Your Right (to Party)."

BREAKTHROUGH

The Beastie Boys' first full-length album, *Licensed to Ill,* was released in November 1986. By March 1987, it was number one on the *Billboard* album charts, the first rap album to reach that position. It was also the biggest selling debut album in the

ROLLING STONE

Rolling Stone magazine was founded in 1967 by Jann Wenner (who is still editor and publisher) and music critic Ralph J. Gleason. It quickly became one of the leading publications of the hippie counterculture era. Famous for its coverage of contemporary popular music, it became equally well-known for its coverage of politics and cultural events and movements. Many well-known writers such as Hunter S. Thompson, Greil Marcus, and Cameron Crowe became famous writing for the magazine.

By the mid-1970s, the magazine was so popular and powerful that the song "Cover of the Rolling Stone" became a hit single for Dr. Hook and the Medicine Show. The song was written by Shel Silverstein—the same Shel Silverstein who wrote the popular childrens books *Where the Sidewalk Ends* and *A Light in the Attic.*

Even today, *Rolling Stone* is considered one of the most powerful magazines in the country. It helps shape what music we listen to, what movies we watch, and what is considered hip and hot.

In 1986, the Beastie Boys released their first full-length album, *Licensed to Ill*, which became number one on the *Billboard* album charts. *Licensed to Ill* was a smash success, becoming the best-selling rap album of the 1980s. Posing with a group of fans are Ad-Rock *(obscured, in cap)*, Mike D *(behind him)*, and MCA *(center)*.

history of Columbia Records. The album's first single, "(You Gotta) Fight for Your Right (to Party)" peaked at number seven on the *Billboard* Hot 100. It quickly became an anthem for college fraternity boys everywhere. The raucous, obnoxious video was played virtually nonstop on MTV.

Plans had long been in the works for a worldwide tour to publicize and help sell the album. The band had initially been booked to play in clubs that held 500 to 700 people. But nobody had anticipated the runaway success of *Licensed to Ill*. By the time the tour reached Houston, Texas, the Beastie Boys were playing to sellout crowds of 18,000 people.

They had become a phenomenon. Their album covered all the topics dear to its target audience: beer, girls, and bad language. In their lyrics and videos, the band played the role of loud, rowdy, drunk frat boys. So, naturally, the public assumed they were nothing more than loud, rowdy, drunk frat boys. Even the media bought into their act. As New York City's *Village Voice* newspaper headlined in its review of *Licensed to Ill*, "Three Jerks Make a Masterpiece."

The "three jerks" were Michael Diamond, a.k.a. (also known as) Mike D; Adam Yauch, a.k.a. MCA and Nathaniel Hornblower; and Adam Horovitz, a.k.a. King Ad-Rock or Ad-Rock. They'd all grown up in New York City and had been friends for years. Together, they had explored the city's hip downtown music scene. They were serious about their music. They were far from being "jerks."

As 1987 wore on, the tour continued, and the B-Boys (as they like to be called) faced a dilemma. Their image, which had started out as a joke, quickly became a reality. Crowds demanded that they live up to their reputation, and they felt obligated to do so. While their image was an essential part of their success, it wasn't totally who they were. It was just one aspect of their personalities. This is not to say that they weren't rowdy and capable of bad behavior. They were, after all, young, mischievous, and rapidly becoming rich and famous. But their fans expected them to be like their image all the time. They soon became uncomfortable with the roles they were expected to play.

By the end of 1987, they felt they had reached the end of the line. As Adam Yauch says, in Alan Light's *The Skills to Pay the Bills*, "We started getting really sick of each other, and sick of being on the road. Even almost sick of the band, what the band represented, kind of ashamed to be a part of it. We decided to take some time apart from each other, and apart from anything having to do with that stuff." The Beastie Boys were nearly ready to call it quits as a band.

In the photograph above, the Beastie Boys (*left to right:* Ad-Rock, Mike D, and MCA) pose with DJ Hurricane at the 1987 Grammy Awards. Nineteen eighty-seven was a good year for the group. Their album *Licensed to Ill* was at the top of the charts, and their first single "Fight for Your Right" became the unofficial party anthem for kids around the country.

Fortunately for Beastie Boys fans everywhere, they didn't. They took a step back, regrouped, and came back even stronger. All six of their major albums, *Licensed to Ill, Paul's Boutique, Check Your Head, Ill Communication, Hello Nasty,* and *To the 5 Boroughs* have been acclaimed by critics as well as by hordes of B-Boys fans. Each of these albums is considered a modern classic.

How did three middle-class Jewish boys from New York go from being musical clowns to becoming one of the most respected and innovative hip-hop groups of the 1990s and beyond, and one of the most influential musical groups of our time?

Growing Up Beastie

All three of the boys who became known as the Beastie Boys grew up in New York City. Their families ranged from middle class to wealthy, and all had parents who were involved in the creative arts.

Adam Yauch is the oldest. He was born on August 5, 1964. His father, Noel, was an architect, and his mother, Frances, was a public school administrator. Yauch lived in the Cobble Hill area of Brooklyn. Despite the B-Boy's fascination with all things Brooklyn, he was the only one of the three born and raised there.

Michael Diamond was born on November 20, 1965. His parents, Harold and Hester Diamond, were prominent New York City art dealers. They lived on the Upper West Side of

Manhattan, in an apartment overlooking Central Park. Michael grew up surrounded by great art. His father died in 1982, and in late 2004, Sotheby's auction house auctioned off six of the paintings he had owned for more than $60 million. One of the paintings was by famed Dutch artist Piet Mondrian; it sold for a record $21 million.

Adam Horovitz is the youngest of the three. He was born on October 31, 1966. He grew up on 11th Street in Greenwich Village in Manhattan. The Village, as it is called, is known for its large population of artists of all kinds. His father is the famous playwright Israel Horovitz, who is best known for his 1968 play, *The Indian Wants the Bronx*, winner of the 1967–1968 Obie Award for distinguished production. (The Obies are awards that are given to plays that appear off Broadway in New York.) The play starred a then little-known actor named Al Pacino, who was also awarded an Obie for his work in the play. Adam Horovitz's parents divorced when he was just three years old. After that, he was mostly raised by his mother, Doris Keefe, a painter who also ran a thrift store. (On an EP by his first group, the Young and the Useless, Adam is listed as "Adam O'Keefe.")

NEW MUSIC

New York City has long been a culturally and creatively inspiring place to live, but its music scene in the late 1970s and early 1980s—when the boys were growing up there—was particularly fertile. Two different types of music were developing and taking shape at that time: In Harlem and the Bronx, black kids on street corners and at block parties were listening to something new, which would become known as hip-hop. DJs such as Kool DJ Herc and Grandmaster Flash began using audio mixers and two records to extend the breaks on funk recordings. This created a more danceable sound. This technique was common in Jamaica, where it was known as dub music. It spread throughout New York by way of the large Jamaican immigrant community.

All three members of the Beastie Boys come from a similar background: Each grew up in New York City, and each was surrounded by the creative arts. In the photograph above, Adam Horovitz poses with his father, the famous playwright Israel Horovitz, who won a 1967–1968 Obie Award for his play *The Indian Wants the Bronx*.

Soon, performers began speaking (or "rapping") during the instrumental breaks. The performers became known as emcees, or MCs. Teams of MCs began springing up throughout the country. Often, these teams were collaborations between former gang members. These teams often emceed for hours at a time. They used some improvisation and a simple four-count beat. There was often a basic chorus between verses that allowed the performer time to gather his thoughts. As time passed, the MCs' raps grew more complicated, incorporating rhymes and using more complicated rhythmic patterns.

By the late 1970s, hip-hop had moved from the streets to the record stores. The first two commercially issued hip-hop recordings, "King Tim III (Personality Jock)" by the Fatback Band and "Rapper's Delight" by the Sugarhill Gang were released in 1979. "Rapper's Delight" actually became a Top 40 hit on the U.S. *Billboard* pop singles chart. Other singles followed, including "The Breaks" by Kurtis Blow, "Funk You Up" by the Sequence, and "The Message" by Grandmaster Flash and the Furious Five. These songs, as well as many others, were very successful. The general feeling, though, was that hip-hop was just another musical novelty. Many people felt that the rap fad would soon die out.

Those predictions were wrong. By the early 1980s, hip-hop had diversified and developed into more complex forms. The early rap styles were replaced with denser, more complicated raps performed over highly complex multilayered beats. Early stars such as Kurtis Blow became mainstream performers. His appearance in a Sprite commercial made him the first hip-hop performer considered mainstream enough to endorse a major product.

Techniques in hip-hop recordings changed as well. Grandmaster Flash's DJ record, "Adventures on the Wheels of Steel" was known for its pioneering use of scratching. Scratching shows off the DJ's skill in manipulating vinyl records to make an assortment of sounds. Almost all scratches are produced by moving a vinyl record back and forth manually while it's playing on a turntable. This creates the distinctive sound that is one of the most recognizable parts of hip-hop music. The technique has spread to other musical genres, including pop, jazz, and even classical.

At the same time that hip-hop was developing in the Bronx and Harlem, a new kind of music was developing along the

Grandmaster Flash was a popular New York DJ who made a name for himself during the late 1970s and early 1980s. He developed the groundbreaking DJ technique of scratching, which is now commonly associated with hip-hop music. In 2007, Grandmaster Flash was the first DJ to be inducted into the Rock and Roll Hall of Fame.

Bowery in Manhattan. It was called punk. During the early 1970s, popular music included disco, heavy metal, progressive rock, and arena rock. Each of these genres was heavily orchestrated, complicated, and highly commercial. Some people felt that this music was bloated compared to rock's early days. They wanted to strip it down to its basics. Punk music set out to do just that.

Punk music has simple musical structures and arrangements. Most songs have a basic verse and chorus and use a simple 4/4 time signature. The songs are normally short, about two and a half minutes long; some are as short as just 30 seconds. Punk songs are known for their simple three-chord arrangements and are generally played very loudly. They are also known for their energy and drive.

Punk sprang up in New York as well as in the U.K. in the years 1974–1976. Early New York bands included the Ramones, the New York Dolls, Television, Blondie, Johnny Thunders and the Heartbreakers, and the Talking Heads. These bands played at New York City clubs such as Max's Kansas City and CBGB. Like hip-hop, punk music grew in popularity. White kids hit the downtown clubs in Mohawk haircuts and leather jackets. They loved the basic jagged and raw sounds of punk.

HIGH SCHOOL

Soon, the worlds of hip-hop and punk began to meet and blend. Downtown clubs like the Roxy began to host hip-hop nights. Art galleries on New York's Lower East Side began to show graffiti as art. Adam Yauch remembers listening to rap early on. "It was around ninth grade when the first rap records came out. We used to listen to those, even when I was into punk and I used to always try to rhyme, like I'd rhyme along with the records," he says in *The Skills to Pay the Bills*.

The pioneering punk group Blondie had a number-one hit in 1981 with "Rapture." The song featured lead singer Debbie Harry's rap. It was the first rap single to reach number one on the charts. It also helped to introduce rap to a white main-stream audience. While the worlds of punk and hip-hop began to marry, punk music itself became more extreme. The sound became even more raw. Punk bands began to compete to see who could play the hardest, fastest, and loudest. This genre became known as hardcore.

This was the musical world that the boys were begin-ning to explore. Though they attended different high schools (Adam Yauch attended Friends Seminary; Mike Diamond was at the well-known Brooklyn private school Saint Ann's; and Adam Horovitz started at Stuyvesant High School and then transferred to the experimental City-as-School program), they would meet at clubs in the Tribeca warehouse district, such as the Mudd Club and the Rock Lounge. The boys got drunk and, according to *Rolling Stone*, "[ran] around the deserted streets with shopping carts."

Adam Yauch had met early Beastie Boys member John Berry at a small punk club called Tier 3. A couple of days

CBGB

CBGB was a legendary music club located at 315 Bowery in New York City. The full name of the club is CBGB & OMFUG, which stands for Country Bluegrass Blues and Other Music for Uplifting Gormandizers. ("Gormandizer" usually means someone who's a ravenous eater of food. But according to CBGB founder Hilly Kristal, in this case, it means a ravenous eater of music.)

After opening in December 1973, it quickly became THE place to hear punk music. Bands such as Television, the Patti Smith Group, Blondie, the Ramones, and the Talking Heads all played its stage. The owners of the club had only one rule for any band playing: They had to play original songs.

In the mid-1980s, the club became a major part of New York City's hardcore scene. Sunday afternoons were dedicated to hardcore. Several bands would take the stage and perform during the afternoon and on into the evening, playing for little or no money.

The club went into a gradual decline and could not afford the skyrocketing neighborhood rents. CBGB held its final concert on October 15, 2006, headlined by punk priestess Patti Smith. Owner Hilly Kristal plans to strip the club down to its bare walls and rebuild it in Las Vegas.

CBGB was a legendary punk-rock club in New York City. During the 1970s and 1980s, CBGB became an institution in the music world, featuring artists such as Blondie, the Ramones, and the Talking Heads. In 2006, the beloved club officially closed it doors.

later, John brought Mike Diamond with him. At that time, John and Mike were in a band called the Young Aborigines. Mike played drums, John played guitar, and Kate Schellenbach played percussion. The four quickly bonded over their mutual love of punk music. They continued exploring the downtown music scene.

It was an easy musical scene to get into. No experience or musical training was necessary. All you needed was energy. As Adam Yauch told *Rolling Stone*, "[The musicians] were people just like you, standing five feet away, and the music was incredible, really powerful. It wasn't like going to see Genesis in some [huge] arena, where some guy who's been studying keyboards for fifteen years is playing "dit-dit-doo-dit-dit-doo."

In 1981, Adam Yauch and Mike Diamond saw the hardcore punk group Black Flag play for the first time. That gave them an idea. As Yauch says in *The Skills to Pay the Bills*, "After we saw Black Flag, we thought we should start a hardcore band. There weren't really any New York hardcore bands [Black Flag was from Washington, D.C.], so we were like, Let's start one, kind of as a joke. And that was called Beastie Boys."

How did they get the name? Some claim that "Beastie" is an acronym for "Boys Entering Anarchistic States Toward Internal Excellence." Mike Diamond offered this explanation in *Rolling Stone*: "When hardcore started, people would come up with stupid names. And it was the stupidest name we could come up with." Early band member Kate Schellenbach had a different story. She claimed that Adam Yauch had been making homemade buttons for different bands. On a whim, he had made a button that said "Beastie Boys." They thought it was so cool that they adopted the name.

Early member John Berry had a different take on the origin of the group's name. He says in *The Skills to Pay the Bills*, "This may be argued, but I think I actually came up with the name. We decided that we should have a gang, an Elks Lodge-type thing. We had secret handshakes and stuff and we'd wear old-man clothes that we'd find at Salvation Army, and we'd smoke cigars. The thrust was pretty much to walk around and annoy people and just be obnoxious. I don't think there was an agenda, really."

Whatever the explanation for the origin of the name, a new group was born.

From Hardcore to Hip-Hop

The original lineup for the Beastie Boys was Adam Yauch on bass; Mike Diamond on vocals; John Berry on guitar; and Kate Schellenbach on drums. The band's first gig was a party at John Berry's house held on Adam Yauch's 17th birthday. It was quite a party. Kate Schellenbach says in *The Skills to Pay the Bills*, "All our friends came and then people who weren't our friends came and there was a fight, someone got beat up and people had to run. Upper West Side kids, downtown kids, Brooklyn kids. And we showed Super 8 films, we had TVs on, we played—it was a multimedia experience."

Although the party may have gotten out of control, the band was a big success. Immediately after the party, they were approached by Dave Parsons from Ratcage Records. He asked them if they would be interested in making a record. The result was an eight-song EP entitled *Polly Wog Stew*. It was released in 1982. Most of the hardcore songs like "Transit Cop" and "Holy Snappers" were fairly forgettable. However, the song "Egg Raid on Mojo" is still played on occasion by the B-Boys in live shows.

The group began performing in clubs, opening for such prominent bands as the Bad Brains. It wasn't long before they began to get noticed. Thurston Moore of the band Sonic Youth says in *The Skills to Pay the Bills*, "The Beastie Boys were one of the bands in the first generation of the New York hardcore scene . . . They were really kids, but they weren't like street-rat kids—they obviously had this edge over everybody else. Their humor was a little more sophisticated; it wasn't just fart-joke humor. Mike D was this skinny kid jumping up in the air and landing on the stage like this screaming little bird or something. They really stood out."

Polly Wog Stew came out during Adam Yauch's senior year in high school. He and Mike Diamond were both ready to go off to college. Other changes were in the works as well. Guitarist John Berry was on his way out of the band. He had begun to use drugs and lost interest in the group. Adam Horovitz was brought in as his replacement.

At the age of fourteen, Adam Horovitz had played in his first band, the Young and the Useless, along with Dave Scilken. Horovitz could play guitar, but not very well. He'd met Adam Yauch at the Rat Cage record shop, where they hung out after cutting class. Even though he could barely play, Horovitz taught Yauch how to play bass. The Young and the Useless had also been signed to Rat Cage Records. They performed Beastie Boys covers on stage. Horovitz was already friends with all the members of Beastie Boys. Adding him to the band was a no-brainer.

The band was scheduled to record a new album, but with Yauch attending Bard College and Mike Diamond at Vassar, there was only time to record one single, called "Cooky Puss." (The flip side of the single was a mock reggae song, "Beastie Revolution.") The name "Cooky Puss" comes from a frozen ice-cream cake made by Carvel Ice Cream. The origins of the song are quite interesting. One day, the guys made a prank phone call to the Carvel toll-free phone number. They recorded the conversation and turned it into a single. It wasn't punk. It wasn't quite rap, either. It was somewhere in between.

The song became a cult hit in 1983. (British Airways used a piece of the track in a commercial without asking permission. The lawsuit that ensued brought the boys their first bit of money and some independence.) College radio stations began to play "Cooky Puss," which led to show bookings. Their live performances were a blend of punk and hip-hop, with Adam Horovitz break-dancing to keep the crowd entertained.

They rented a floor under a sweatshop in New York's Chinatown, where they could live and rehearse. The floor of the apartment was blacktop. The ceiling leaked. The sound of the factory machinery could be heard at all hours. Life under a sweatshop definitely wasn't easy. Once, the boys were hanging out in the living room and heard an explosion in the kitchen. Upon examination, they found holes in their wall, ceiling, and even their toaster oven. It turned out that someone upstairs had fired a gun through the floor. The shot had gone through the toaster and right into the wall! The upside of their place was that they could play their music as loud as they wanted to, whenever they wanted to. They had easy access to all the downtown clubs. Living beneath a Chinatown sweatshop allowed them to live the life of downtown rockers.

RICK RUBIN AND DEF JAM

"Cooky Puss" was soon heard by a young New York University student named Rick Rubin, who changed the boys' lives forever. Rubin is one of America's best-known record producers. During his career, he has worked with such varied artists as

In this 1985 photograph, the Beastie Boys pose with music producer Rick Rubin *(third from the left)*. When he was a college student at NYU, Rubin formed Def Jam Recordings with Russell Simmons. The Beastie Boys became a part of Def Jam Recordings, and Rick Rubin served as their original DJ.

LL Cool J, Stryker, Jay-Z, the Dixie Chicks, Justin Timberlake, System of a Down, Johnny Cash, and Tom Petty. Today, he is best known for his work with the Red Hot Chili Peppers. MTV has called him "the most important producer of the last 20 years."

Early in his career, he was a major figure in fusing the worlds of rap and hard rock. His recording of "Walk This Way" featured a collaboration between rap stars Run-DMC and rock stars Aerosmith. The resulting classic recording is credited with introducing rap–hard rock (also called rapcore) to mainstream audiences.

Rick Rubin was a white fan of heavy metal who grew up in Long Island. He did some deejaying at local clubs and had his own hard rock band. Fascinated early on with hip-hop, he started mixing his own tapes, blending hard rock and hip-hop to create new sounds. It was through his interest in hip-hop that he met Russell Simmons.

Russell Simmons is the older brother of Run-DMC member Joseph "Run" Simmons. Russell grew up in Hollis, an African-American neighborhood of Queens, New York. Like many in his neighborhood, he started out by selling illegal drugs; however, he quickly realized how risky that kind of life could be. As a college student, he began promoting hip-hop shows. He also managed then up-and-coming hip-hop artists like Kurtis Blow. When he met Rick Rubin through mutual friends, they instantly clicked. They began a musical partnership that helped to bring hip-hop music into the mainstream. Their company was called Def Jam records.

Rubin first hooked up with the Beastie Boys when he was still a student at New York University. Along with his studies, he chaired a social committee at NYU, deejayed, and, along with Russell Simmons, ran Def Jam Records out of his dorm room. Rubin and Simmons had a similar vision for the company. Rubin wanted to find a group that could make rap records with a hard-rock drive. Simmons wanted to find a group that had the energy of a street party and would be popular with as large an audience as possible. They found their ideal band in the Beastie Boys.

The group started hanging out with Rubin. They wanted to emcee in their live shows and needed a DJ to do so, and Rubin was the only guy they knew with all the turntables and equipment they needed. As Cey Adams, long-time friend and designer of the cover for the B-Boy's album *Hello Nasty*, remembers it in *The Skills to Pay the Bills*, "Rick would take us out. He was the only one we knew at the time who had money that could feed everybody. Rick picking up the tab played a big part in us hanging out with him." Under Rubin's influence, the group gradually changed from a punk rock outfit to a rap crew.

Kate Schellenbach was soon out of the group. She was a rocker, not a rapper. She didn't get along with Rick Rubin, and Rick Rubin didn't feel that having a woman in the group fit his image for the band. Schellenbach later went on to join the group Luscious Jackson in 1991.

Under Rubin's guidance, the band returned to the studio, where they recorded the 12-inch single "Rock Hard." ("Rock Hard" sampled AC/DC's "Back in Black." The song is now out of print and considered a rare collector's item. The Beastie Boys wanted to include it on their 1999 anthology, *The Sounds of Science*, but AC/DC refused to allow the sample to be used.) By now, the boys had acquired their professional names: Mike D, MCA, and King Ad-Rock.

The Beastie Boys were ready to show themselves to the world as rappers. According to *Rolling Stone*, Russell Simmons told them, "You're going to be the most successful group ever." To make that statement a reality, they'd have to play for more than their usual white downtown audiences. They'd have to introduce themselves to black audiences in rap clubs scattered throughout the city and prove themselves worthy of being called "rappers."

PROVING THEMSELVES

As Ad-Rock remembers in *Beastie Boys . . . In Their Own Words*, "I remember going one night doing a gig in a real tough part of town with Kurtis Blow and it was touch and go whether we were going to get out alive. We (got) stared at like we were from outer space, which was a little disconcerting. In that kind of situation, you have to be good at what you do or you're going to be dead." Playing to real hip-hop fans forced the boys to get better—fast. Although their first few concerts didn't go well,

The Beastie Boys are photographed with their Def Jam label mates, Run-DMC. The Beastie Boys' association with Run-DMC and Def Jam gave them credibility with black audiences and hip-hop fans. From left are Mike D, Jam Master Jay, Ad-Rock, Run *(kneeling)*, MCA, and DMC. The Beastie Boys' DJ stands at the top.

they gradually began to earn a loyal audience. They also began to win the respect of other hip-hop artists.

Russell Simmons was eager for his Def Jam label mates Run-DMC, one of the first major rap groups, and the Beastie Boys to get along. Darryl McDaniels (DMC) remembers their first meeting in *The Skill to Pay the Bills*: "Russell was like, 'Yo, when you meet these guys, they're gonna bug you out. These white guys are ill' . . . the thing about 'em was that they were so real. It wasn't like a bunch of white guys faking just to be down with hip-hoppers or trying to play a role. I respected that a lot . . . They came off just like somebody I grew up with on my block . . . And they knew a lot about hip-hop, knew about flavor and all that stuff."

Other black hip-hop artists felt the same way. Chuck D of Public Enemy says in *The Skill to Pay the Bills*, "The Beastie Boys came out to our radio show at WBAU, trying to prove

RUN-DMC

Run-DMC was a hip-hop group founded by Joseph "Run" Simmons, Darryl "DMC" McDaniels, and the late Jason "Jam Master Jay" Mizell. They had an enormous impact on the development of hip-hop throughout the 1980s. They are also credited with helping to introduce hip-hop into mainstream music.

All three members of the group grew up in the Hollis neighborhood of Queens, New York. "Run" Simmons is the brother of Russell Simmons. He entered the hip-hop scene by deejaying for one of his brother's first big acts—Kurtis Blow. Run recruited his best friend and gifted rhymer Darryl McDaniels to join him onstage. The two began performing and soon brought in Jam Master Jay to complete the trio.

In 1983, they released their first single, "It's Like That," and they were soon discovered by MTV. They became the very first rap group to have a video played on MTV. Their debut album, *Run-D.M.C.*, was the first rap album to go gold. In addition, they had the first rap album to go to number one on the R&B charts. They were popular for more than their music. They set new clothing trends by performing in baggy black clothing, Adidas sneakers (with the shoelaces removed), and fedora hats.

to the rap market that they were viable white kids. You really couldn't doubt their legitimacy, 'cause they were down with Def Jam and Run-DMC. The beats were right, and at that time, it didn't take much skill to ride the beats. It was a simpler style and a different time. And as long as they talked about white boys and beer and stuff like that, who could knock their topics?"

Mainstream success continued when the group released their 1986 album, *Raising Hell*, which quickly became the highest-selling rap album in history. (This record has since been broken by artists such as Notorious B.I.G. and Eminem.) *Raising Hell* contained what is perhaps their most famous song, a collaboration with the rock group Aerosmith on that group's classic song "Walk This Way." The collaboration was the first hip-hop song to make the Top 10 on *Billboard*'s singles charts.

The band is legendary for breaking new ground in rap music. The songs "It's Like That" and "Sucker MC's" were the first hip-hop songs that relied on electronic beats and nothing else. "Peter Piper" was the first rap record in which the DJ cut up a record.

The band suffered a tragic loss on October 30, 2002, when Jam Master Jay was shot and killed in a recording studio in Queens, New York. The murder still has not been solved. Since then, Darryl "DMC" McDaniels has released his first solo album, *Checks, Thugs and Rock N Roll*. Joseph "Run" Simmons released a solo album as well and currently stars in the MTV reality show *Run's House*.

Their place on Def Jam records alongside Run-DMC increased their credibility with black audiences. Like Eminem working with Dr. Dre years later, it gave them instant legitimacy that might have taken them years to earn on their own.

It was obvious to all that the group respected and knew hip-hop. One day Rick Rubin received a demo tape from a previously unknown artist. Rubin wasn't impressed with it, but Ad-Rock encouraged him to sign the young man, and he did. The young man's name was James Todd Smith III. His stage name was LL Cool J, and he went on to become one of the biggest rap stars of all time. (Ad-Rock was one of the writers of LL's first single, "I Need a Beat.")

MADONNA

What happened next was perhaps the biggest break in the group's career. Madonna was about to start her first tour and needed an opening act. According to MCA, Madonna contacted Russell Simmons to ask whether the Fat Boys—a popular hip-hop trio whose best-known member, Buffy the Human Beatbox, is credited with pioneering beatboxing—were available. Simmons didn't manage the Fat Boys, but rather than admit that, he told Madonna that they were already booked. He then offered her Run-DMC, but they were too expensive for the pop star. So Simmons offered her a good deal on the Beastie Boys, and she accepted. The boys had never met Madonna, but they all had hung out at the same New York City clubs, such as Danceteria. They all knew of each other, and they knew each other's music.

The Beastie Boys had one problem to settle before the tour began. They only had three songs of their own to perform: "Slow and Low," "Beastie Groove," and "Rock Hard." They quickly went into the studio to record a new single, "She's on It." Those four songs, along with a cover version of T LaRock's "It's Yours" gave them enough material to open a concert.

It turned out that there was one more problem for the B-Boys. The crowds hated them. At that stage of her career, Madonna was appealing to mostly preteen and teenage white girls. They dressed like her, knew all her songs, and wanted to be just like her. The last thing they wanted to see on stage was three white male hip-hop artists rapping about beer and girls.

They were booed every night. Audiences did not understand the Beastie Boys' humor. They were offended by their lyrics and did not want to see them onstage grabbing their crotches, drinking beer, and running around the stage like madmen. Many in Madonna's management team wanted her to fire them from the tour, but Madonna stood by them. She believed that their music was ahead of its time and that, eventually, people would understand what the B-Boys were doing and embrace them.

Others agreed. Bill Adler, who was publicist for Def Jam Records, says in *The Skills to Pay the Bills*, "They were booed the entire time. When I saw that, I thought, These guys are great. They're gonna be fine." He knew that if they could proudly play their music, despite the crowd's reaction, that they could survive anything.

Despite the crowds' reaction, the boys were having the time of their lives. They were playing to huge crowds. They were getting to play the music they loved, and, as it turned out, they loved playing on stage. Ad-Rock, especially, due to his family background in theater, knew how to use the stage to project the image he wanted. In *The Skill to Pay the Bills*, he remembers, "It was totally ridiculous. It was great. It was great. They hated us so much. It was the most bizarrest thing to be playing in these huge places—Radio City Music Hall for, like two, three nights. I don't understand what happened. It was just bananas." They knew, though, that even if 95 percent of the crowd hated them, another 5 percent loved them, and it was that 5 percent that would become their fan base.

In 1985, the Beastie Boys were the opening act for Madonna during her Virgin Tour. Although the group was not well received by Madonna's fans, the Beastie Boys had the time of their lives on tour. They had the opportunity to play music in front of large crowds, and they didn't mind getting a negative reaction from the audience.

RAISING HELL

After Madonna's Virgin tour had finished, the boys went back on the road. This time though, the tour was a better fit for their music. Headlined by Run-DMC, the tour was called Raising Hell and also featured Whodini, the Timex Social Club, and LL Cool J. Being on tour with these groups allowed the boys to be taken seriously as hip-hop artists.

On the Raising Hell tour, the Beastie Boys were in their element. The crowds loved them. It didn't matter to the audience whether the group was white or black, as long as they could rap, and that they could do. Hip-hop fans knew that they were the real thing.

As DMC says in *The Skills to Pay the Bills*, "From day one, they was killing. Even when nobody knew them, they was killing. It could be a completely black, Negro, southern crowd, here to see Run-DMC and Whodini and their favorites. But when the Beasties came on, it wasn't like people were walking around getting hot dogs; they really paid attention to those white boys. What was cool about 'em, I never had to defend them. None of the hardcore hip-hoppers would come up and say, 'Now why are you on the tour with them fake white boys?' or anything. We never got anything negative . . . Because I'm telling you, all the homies were like, Those kids are ill, man."

Of course a few people disagreed. They felt that since the B-Boys didn't come from the streets of the Bronx or Harlem, that they hadn't paid their dues. Some suggested that the only reason the group was invited to tour with Run-DMC was because they were white, not because they were good. They felt that white rappers had no place in black hip-hop culture. Even pioneering white rapper MC Serch thought that they were the worst thing that could happen to hip-hop; however, he was in a minority.

Russell Simmons's strategy was correct. He knew that to sell the Beastie Boys as a hip-hop group, he first had to sell them to a black audience. To be accepted by black audiences, they would have to be authentic talents. Then, after confirming their legitimacy, it would be easy to sell them to a white audience.

Because of the exposure they received on tour, their single "Hold It Now, Hit It" made *Billboard*'s national R&B and Dance charts. Their double A-side 12-inch "Paul Revere/The New Style" was released at the end of 1985 and became another R&B/Dance hit. It was clear that the Beastie Boys were ready to take the next step: It was time for them to record their first full-length album.

LICENSED TO ILL

They worked on their album throughout 1986. Songs were written on the tour bus and in the studio. Initially, they were in no hurry to finish, but with the success of "Hold It Now, Hit It," pressure began to come from Columbia/CBS Records, which distributed records for Def Jam. They felt that since they now had a hit single, a new album should come out as soon as possible.

Recording the album was more relaxed than one might imagine. The boys spent the night dancing and partying at clubs like Danceteria and Area. Then, late at night, they'd go to the recording studio. The studio was called Chung King, and it was located in New York's Chinatown. At the studio, the group feasted on big bags of White Castle burgers, along with beer and Coca-Cola. People constantly wandered in and out; even Adam Horovitz's mom stopped by to lend her support.

Just before the album was released, there was one problem to resolve: Rick Rubin, Ad-Rock, and MCA were considering kicking Mike D out of the band. Apparently, they questioned whether Mike was what they called "Beastie Down" enough; they thought Mike D's sound was too "white" or "downtown" to fit in with the rest of the group. There were other, more personal, issues as well: While Rick Rubin and Ad-Rock had become close friends, and MCA and Ad-Rock had roomed together, in some ways, Mike D was the odd man out. Ultimately, loyalty won out, and they decided Mike should stay.

Having cemented their commitment, the group was ready to release *Licensed to Ill*. Nobody involved with the group could have guessed how successful the album would be. With its release, "Beastiemania" was about to sweep the country.

Fame and Its Aftermath

Licensed to Ill came out in late 1986 and received terrific reviews. Jayson Young of "Rap Reviews" wrote, "The way these boys trade lines, and even sometimes individual words, is almost unequaled by anyone. One of the tightest teams in all of hip-hop . . . *Licensed to Ill* should be in every true head's collection, no excuses."

Rolling Stone magazine listed it at #217 of the top 500 albums of all time and called *Licensed to Ill* "a revolutionary combination of hip-hop beats, metal riffs, and some of the most exuberant, unapologetic smart-aleck rhymes ever made."

Stephen Thomas Erlewine of All Music summed up the album nicely, "There hasn't been a funnier, more infectious record in pop music than this . . . there is the overpowering loudness of the record—operating from the axis of where metal, punk, and rap meet, there has never been a record this heavy and nimble . . . *Licensed to Ill* reigns tall among the greatest records of its time."

The album is a marvel. It has a hard rock swagger and the clever and insolent rhymes of rap at its best. There is also the use of sampling: Pieces of music from the rock group Led Zeppelin, the funk group War, and even the theme song from the TV show *Mr. Ed* all found their way onto the album. The wide variety of musical sources adds enormous sonic depth and interest to the music.

Licensed to Ill was completed just before digital sampling had become possible, so it was done literally with tape loops. (In looping, a length of recorded magnetic tape is cut and spliced end to end. This creates a circle or loop that can be played continuously to create a repetitive rhythmic musical pattern.) For example, the beat for "When the Levee Breaks" (used in the song "Rhymin' and Stealin'") was recorded on quarter-inch tape. They made a loop of that beat on a long, continuous piece of tape. The tape was so long that it would go around the room, hanging off mic stands in a giant loop.

Licensed to Ill also stood out for its use of cultural references. Treasure Island and Betty Crocker. Pablo Picasso and Bullwinkle the Moose. Kentucky Fried Chicken and Paul Revere. Chef Boyardee and Rice-A-Roni. All of these and more found their way into the B-Boy's lyrics.

Songs like "No Sleep 'Til Brooklyn," "Slow and Low," "Paul Revere," "Hold It Now, Hit It," and "Girls" show off the Beastie Boys at their best. They showcase their humor and their ability to trade off rhymes and build interesting musical landscapes. Ironically though, it was a throwaway single, "(You Gotta) Fight for Your Right (to Party)," that became the group's biggest hit.

The Beastie Boys' debut album, *Licensed to Ill*, received rave reviews and sold more than 5 million copies. The album featured the hit songs "(You Gotta) Fight for Your Right (to Party)" and "No Sleep 'Til Brooklyn." In the photograph above, the group promotes their music on *The Joe Franklin Show* in 1986.

YOU GOTTA FIGHT

To Mike D, MCA, and King Ad-Rock, the song was nothing more than a joke. When Rick Rubin heard it though, he saw different musical possibilities. Rubin added big loud rock guitars and straight-ahead rock drumming to the track. With that bit of tweaking, it became the obvious song to release as a single.

To go along with the single, a video was required. The inspiration for the video was, surprisingly enough, the party scene in the 1962 movie *Breakfast at Tiffany's*. In the movie, the scene is a classic 1960s-style cocktail party. In the B-Boy's video,

MTV

At 12:01 A.M., on August 1, 1981, television history was made. With the announcement "Ladies and Gentlemen, rock and roll!" and the playing of "Video Killed the Radio Star," MTV (Music Television) was born.

Watching MTV today, it's hard to believe that the station once played nothing but music videos, 24 hours a day. Many successful rock bands and performers of the 1980s became famous because of MTV. Acts like the Police, the Eurythmics, Duran Duran, Bon Jovi, Michael Jackson, Madonna, and of course the Beastie Boys became stars in large part because of the play their videos received on MTV.

In recent years, MTV's programming has shifted from music videos to original shows. Cartoons like *Beavis and Butthead*; reality shows like *The Real World*, *The Osbournes*, *Newlyweds*, and *Laguna Beach* and dating shows such as *Next* and *Parental Control* have come to dominate MTV programming. Music videos can be seen at certain times, and on shows like *TRL*, but less often than previously.

What many people don't realize is that MTV is not just American; it's a global phenomenon. Countries such as Portugal, Finland, Italy, Romania, Japan, China, Philippines, India, Brazil, and Russia all have their own MTV, with local artists and programming, in each country's native language. Some programming, though, is imported from the United States.

it's a nerd gathering turned chaotic party, complete with gags and pies in the face. (Rick Rubin appears in the video, wearing a Slayer T-shirt.)

Both the single and video were huge hits. The single made it to number seven on the *Billboard* charts. The video had a continuous presence on MTV. "(You Gotta) Fight for Your Right (to Party)" was later named by the Rock and Roll Hall of Fame as one of "the 500 Songs that Shaped Rock and Roll."

The Beastie Boys grew to resent the success of the song. The song, after all, had been meant as a joke, but because of the runaway success of the song and video, the boys were stereotyped as the kind of characters they had intended to lampoon. In the liner notes for their 1999 compilation, *The Sounds of Science*, they even apologized for the song. They said that it was meant as a goof on songs like a "Smokin' in the Boys Room" and "I Wanna Rock." Unfortunately, the song and video defined the Beastie Boys in the public's mind for years to come. As Mike D said in January 1987, as quoted in *The Beastie Boys . . . In Their Own Words*, "A lot of the humor wasn't interpreted in a way that we might perhaps have envisaged." The boys never quite imagined that the song would be taken seriously.

Because of the success of the single, sales of the album took off as well. *Licensed to Ill* ultimately sold over 5 million copies. It became the first rap album to reach number one on the pop charts, and it stayed on top for a remarkable seven weeks. The album's release benefited from being perfectly in synch with an explosion in the popularity of hip-hop. Suddenly, hip-hop was everywhere. Hip-hop fashion, such as Adidas sneakers with untied laces, was seen in malls nationwide. MTV introduced its first rap show, *Yo! MTV Raps*.

With success came controversy. Parental groups spoke out against the Beastie Boys' music. They thought their rude, funny lyrics would encourage listeners to take drugs, to become violent, and to treat women badly. The Beastie Boys always made

MTV Music Television debuted on August 1, 1981, and changed the way people were able to access music. With the emergence and popularity of rap music, MTV created *Yo! MTV Raps* in 1988, which solely featured rap music. Above, the Beastie Boys appear on the popular rap show in 1992.

the case that their lyrics were supposed to be funny. They were, they said, making fun of the typical rap lyrics of the time. Still, many people took them and their lyrics seriously, but as MCA said in January 1987, according to *Beastie Boys ... In Their Own Words*, "When we're talking about women or whatever we're creating a fantasy. What we're doing is creating a fantasy, so far-fetched and overboard that the 99 percent of the people that understand it understand that there is such a thing as humor, such a thing as parody."

Criticism came from some black rappers, as well, who for years had tried to get their music played on traditionally white rock stations. They felt that their music had the right attitude and energy and that rock fans would listen to it as if it were rock. The stations, though, refused to play their music. When Beastie Boys came along, rock stations jumped at the chance to play their music. Some rappers felt that this showed that racism was still alive in American music. What was the difference in music, they asked, between the Beastie Boys and Run-DMC? Were the stations playing the Beastie Boys only because the band members were white?

Regardless of the reasons, the Beastie Boys appealed to both the traditional hip-hop audiences and suburban white kids. Black and Hispanic kids responded to the Beasties' nods to hip-hop's musical traditions. White kids related to their rebellious attitude and wiseacre humor.

Bill Stephney, former head of Def Jam Records, says in *The Skills to Pay the Bills,* "Did anyone think it would be the number-one album in the country? Nobody was thinking that . . . I just remember seeing a black and Latino crowd just go crazy, as much over 'The New Style' as over the backwards beat of 'Paul Revere.' You don't have to be a rocket scientist or develop websites to understand that when a white group has that sort of organic core black influence, something can happen."

LIFE ON THE ROAD

Based on the phenomenal success of *Licensed to Ill,* the group began a worldwide tour of the same name in 1987. The Licensed to Ill tour was a huge financial success, but by the time it was all over, the group had nearly called it quits.

For Adam Yauch, Adam Horovitz, and Michael Diamond, the success of their album and hit singles was totally unexpected. With the success came money, fame, and all the perks of being a celebrity. For many, the initial rush of fame can be hard to deal with. Earning too much money too fast and having too many people telling them they're great can change people. It's easy for many young performers to believe the hype and forget who they really are.

Going on tour was a wild experience for the group. Previously they had been an opening act, generally playing in smaller venues. Now they were the stars, playing in giant arenas to tens of thousands of screaming fans. The fans came to see the group they knew from "Fight for Your Right." They wanted to see the loud, obnoxious rappers they loved on the album. For the Beastie Boys, they had meant it all to be a joke. On the Licensed to Ill tour, the joke became reality.

They were as outrageous as they wanted to be. Did they want girls dancing in cages on stage? They got them. Did they want gigantic obscene props decorating the stage? They had them. Did they want to drink beer throughout their concerts? They did it. Originally, they meant it to mock typical rock-star behavior, but because the crowds loved it, the boys began living the roles they were playing on stage. Drinking, partying, and a steady stream of girls became a normal part of their lives.

Eventually, the boys began to tire of the scene, so as the tour went on, they found new ways to amuse themselves. On some nights, they would be their own opening act. But instead of doing it as the Beastie Boys, they came on stage as a different band they called Triphammer. They came out wearing wigs and costumes so they wouldn't be recognized. In this disguise, they played heavy metal, similar to that of Black Sabbath.

Their shows owed a lot to the punk rock scene, with outrageous behavior on stage imitated by the audience. While touring in England, the band was falsely accused by the London tabloid press of insulting some physically disabled fans. Outrage spread throughout the country as members of Parliament tried

The 1987 Licensed to III tour was a wild time for the Beastie Boys. The tour allowed the group to go crazy. With girls in cages and obscene stage props, the tour was one continuous party. Their shows featured outrageous behavior, which their audiences expected.

to expel the band from the country. Angry groups of people protested outside their concerts. People threw cans and spit on them at a concert in Liverpool. The boys were appalled that things could so quickly go out of control. Ad-Rock even spent the weekend in jail after the Liverpool concert. He was charged with assault after a girl claimed she was hit by a beer can that he had thrown back at the audience. Charges were later dropped after the girl stated she had not seen Ad-Rock doing it.

The pressures of touring and simply of being the Beastie Boys began to become too much for the boys. At the time, Ad-Rock was dating actress Molly Ringwald. Whenever he could, he would fly back to California to be with her. He was also thinking about being in movies himself. By the end of the tour, the boys were sick of everything. They were tired of touring. They were tired of playing the roles of drinking, partying Beastie Boys. They were even beginning to hate each other.

RECOVERY AND REGROUPING

MCA called his old friend Kate Schellenbach to share his feelings about what was going on with the group. He told her that he was sick of Rick Rubin and the Beastie Boys, and that he wanted to do something else. Schellenbach walked away from the conversation with the sense that the band wouldn't be together much longer.

MCA put together a new band called Brooklyn. They played just one concert, at the World in New York. The group had a classic rock sound, described as sounding like Bachman-Turner-Overdrive. Ad-Rock was getting offers to be in movies. Mike D had his own projects to consider.

There were other things pulling apart the bandmates, as well. The boys were having problems with Rick Rubin and Def Jam Records. They felt that they were being treated unfairly by Def Jam and that the label was withholding $2 million in royalties that rightfully belonged to them. Russell Simmons claimed that the boys had broken their contract and owed Def Jam another record. He wanted a new record as soon as possible.

The boys, though, were exhausted from touring. They were not sure if they even wanted to be a band anymore. Going into the studio and making a new record was the last thing they wanted to do. They felt that they needed a chance to rest, to regroup, and to recharge their creative batteries. They also felt that Rick Rubin was getting all the credit for their success. Many people outside the group thought that Rubin was the creative force behind the band and that the band could not survive without him. The boys resented this. They knew that the music was their creation, and they felt that Rubin and Def Jam were taking too much of the credit for themselves.

It was all too much for them. They decided they wanted out of their contract with Rick Rubin and Def Jam. If they were ever going to make a new record, it would have to be with somebody else.

The Making
of a
Masterpiece

Getting out of the contract with Def Jam would not be easy. It would take time and effort to find a legal way out. The Beastie Boys wouldn't be able to do it individually, however. The first thing that would have to happen was for the boys to get together again.

At first, that was easier said than done. Ad-Rock was in Los Angeles making the movie *Lost Angels*, in which he played a troubled youth. MCA was busy recording demos in New York with his other band, Brooklyn. Mike D was busy with his jazz band, Big Fat Love and the Flophouse Society Orchestra. How would they be able to work together?

The friendship between the boys proved unbreakable. MCA and Mike D made several trips to Los Angeles to visit Ad-Rock.

The Beastie Boys often performed with their Def Jam label mates Run-DMC. Above, DMC trades lines with Ad-Rock at Seattle's Paramount Theater in 1987. After much conflict with Def Jam and Rick Rubin, the Beastie Boys decided to leave their old label and sign with Capitol Records.

After spending time hanging out together, they realized that they wanted to make music again. Then, through their mutual friend Matt Dike, they hooked up with soon-to-be legendary music producers the Dust Brothers.

The Dust Brothers are Michael "E.Z. Mike" Simpson and John "King Gizmo" King. They had been DJs who hosted what was claimed to be the first all hip-hop radio show in California.

They were also masters of the art of sampling, taking small samples of previously recorded songs and combining them to make incredibly dense and complicated musical backgrounds.

The sampling done on *Licensed to Ill* had been relatively simple and uncomplicated, but the technology had improved since that album was recorded. With the new digital sampling, the Dust Brothers were able to easily obtain, loop, and manipulate small bits and breaks from other songs and put them together, or layer them, to make one song. They raised sampling to new levels; they made it into an art form.

When the B-Boys heard some of the Dust Brothers' work, they immediately knew that they wanted to collaborate with them. They recorded two songs, "Full Clout" and "Car Thief," over previously compiled Dust Brothers tracks. Everybody was amazed at how great they sounded. Now all the boys needed was a new record label.

MOVING TO CAPITOL

In 1988, Dave Carr was living in New York City and was head of Capitol Record's East Coast Records. Only 29 years old, he was a fan of both New York's downtown music scene and hip-hop. When he was asked if he'd be interested in signing the Beastie Boys to Capitol he jumped at the chance. For him, it was a perfect musical match.

However, he had heard the rumors of a Beastie Boys breakup. He had read that Ad-Rock wanted to make a career of acting. Before Carr tried to convince the heads of the company to sign the group, he needed to know that they were going to stay together.

Ad-Rock quickly reassured him. As he remembers in *The Skills to Pay the Bills*, he told Carr, "I just want you to know one thing. Nothing is more important to me in my life than the Beastie Boys. Music is what I'm about. And if you don't think I'm dedicated to this, I just need to tell you that this is the most important thing. And we're gonna make this work. And we're gonna always do it. We're gonna always be on top. And the three of us are inseparable."

Dave Carr was convinced. Now all he had to do was convince the other executives at the company. The Beastie Boys' reputation had preceded them. There were concerns that they were nothing but one-hit wonders. (A one-hit wonder is a group or solo artist that has just one popular song and then never has another.) The legendary stories about their wild behavior on tour were also a concern. In addition, everyone believed that Rick Rubin had actually written their songs and made them who they were. Finally, and perhaps most importantly, there was the issue of the group's contract with Def Jam.

The boys had to fly back out to Los Angeles to prove themselves to the executives at Capitol Records. When they did, they were on their very best behavior. They assured the executives that their attorneys would have no problem getting them out of their Def Jam contract. Growing up in the social circles they had, they knew how to behave properly when it was necessary. For example, when Mike D met the chief executive officer of Capitol Records, Joe Smith, he walked into the meeting and said, according to the book *Paul's Boutique*, "You know, you bought a Brach from my father." (Paul Henry Brach is a noted American Expressionist painter.) Needless to say, Joe Smith was impressed.

The Beastie Boys impressed everyone they needed to impress. As Capitol Records president David Berman says in the book *Paul's Boutique*, "They were, without a doubt, the smartest bunch of really arrogant kids I had ever met. I was like, 'They're too smart not to pull it off.'"

They soon signed a deal with Capitol Records. Compared to the less than $100,000 in royalties they'd received from Def Jam for *Licensed to Ill*, they received a two-album deal worth $3 million. They would also receive advances (money paid to an artist in advance of the work being finished) of $750,000 each.

The signing with Capitol began a year-long legal struggle with Def Jam. Lawsuits were filed by both Def Jam and CBS Records. These suits, filed in both state and federal court, claimed that these labels still had the Beasties under contract. The Beastie Boys quickly struck back. They countersued, claiming breach of contract as well as breach of fiduciary duty. They demanded the money that they believed was owed to them.

The suits were ultimately settled. The Beastie Boys agreed to give up the royalties they claimed were owed to them. In return, Def Jam agreed that they no longer had legal claims to the group. The boys were now free of Def Jam and Rick Rubin.

MAKING *PAUL'S BOUTIQUE*

The band quickly established base at the Mondrian Hotel in Los Angeles, California, on Sunset Boulevard. Armed with $750,000 each, they began a year of serious partying. Ad-Rock started dating actress Ione Skye, daughter of folk singer Donovan. MCA was doing a lot of skiing. There were frequent pool parties. There were road trips exploring Southern California. There were nights of partying. Los Angeles had a lot of distractions for young rock stars with a lot of money.

The boys also had fun pulling pranks. Across the street from the Mondrian was the Comedy Store, a well-known comedy club. People often stood in line waiting to get into the club each night. Unable to resist such a target, the boys and their friends lobbed eggs out their hotel room windows across the street into the waiting crowds. According to *Spin* magazine, the boys soon received a letter from the Mondrian's management. It said something like, "We've had some reports of things falling out of your window. If there's a problem with your window, please let us know."

No longer able to throw eggs out of their window, they got into their cars and threw eggs at random people and buildings they passed. This activity even inspired a new song, "Egg Man."

They were having a lot of fun, but when were they working on the album? As Mike D told a radio interviewer in 1989, according to the book *Paul's Boutique*, "It would be great, you know, if we could all just go to work every day and say, OK, we're gonna work in the studio from one o'clock until dah-dah-dah, and we're gonna finish the album in two months. But it never works like that . . . You might go for two weeks and get one day of work done. But that one day of work is very special, for very special people like ourselves."

The early work on the album was slow. Partying all night made getting up in the morning impossible. Afternoons were supposed to be dedicated to writing. There was another problem: Doubt had begun to set in. The boys were no longer sure what it was they wanted to do. As Mike D pointed out in the book *Paul's Boutique*, this was not an uncommon occurrence. "On every record we've had that. We sit down and we look at each other: 'OK, what . . . are we gonna say now?'"

Pressure began to mount from Capitol Records to finish the record. Realizing that they needed to buckle down and get to work, they knew that they would have to make some changes. They moved from the Mondrian Hotel to a rented house. The house was known as the G Spot and was frequently rented to celebrities. Mike D took over the master suite. MCA settled into the video room. Ad-Rock moved into the underground bedroom in the guest house. This room had a window looking directly into the swimming pool. In the inner sleeve of *Paul's Boutique* there is an underwater photo of the B-Boys swimming. The photo was taken from the window of Ad-Rock's bedroom.

After the move, the work came together fairly quickly. The technical work of layering and looping to synchronize perfectly was a difficult challenge. Today, the work is easy to do with a computer. In 1988, what today takes just a few minutes took hours to do. Mike Simpson described the process in the book *Paul's Boutique*: "Basically, we would find a groove, and we would loop it, and then we would print that tape, and we would

Following the Licensed to Ill tour, the boys split up and worked on their own projects. Adam Horovitz tried his hand at acting and starred in the 1989 film *Lost Angels* opposite film legend Donald Sutherland *(above right)*. Because his music was more important to him, he soon put aside acting to concentrate on the Beastie Boys.

just go for five minutes on one track of the tape. And then we would find another loop, and we would spend hours getting the second loop to sync (match) up with the first loop . . . It was just painful. It took so long."

It is estimated that between 100 and 300 samples were used in *Paul's Boutique*. (The name of the album was taken from a radio ad on one of Ad-Rock's reggae cassettes. The Brooklyn store supposedly sold "the best in men's clothing.") The song "Shake Your Rump" for example contains at least fifteen different samples. "Egg Man," a song that clocks in at under three minutes, includes at least 14 different samples. Everything from the Beatles, Kurtis Blow, the Ramones, Isaac Hayes, the Jackson 5, Bob Marley, Elvis Costello, and the theme to the movie *Jaws* were used to create the album's signature sound.

Mike D described the sound to writer Chris Morris in a 1989 *Billboard* magazine article: "You could use the word, maybe 'stew,' or 'pot luck dinner,' or 'casserole,' those type of terms. What you're talking about is, you're combining a lot of different things, a lot of different seasonings."

The music served as an ideal base for the Beasties' lyrics. In *Paul's Boutique* the lyrics were less juvenile; the humor was more sophisticated. They were moving from being teenagers to adults, and it showed.

Their love of references to popular culture continued. TV shows like *The Patty Duke Show* and *The Brady Bunch*; legendary rock stars like Bob Dylan and David Bowie; and figures as different as Donald Trump, Sir Isaac Newton, explorer Ponce de Leon, and famous author Jack Kerouac make appearances in the B-Boy's lyrics. Look at these lines from the song "Shadrach": "Got more stories than JD got Salinger / I hold the title and you are the challenger / I've got money like Charles Dickens / Got the girlies in the Coupe like the Colonel's got chickens." American author J.D. Salinger, English novelist Charles Dickens, Cadillac Coupe de Ville, and KFC's Colonel Sanders are all referenced in just four short lines. To the Beastie Boys, anything and anyone throughout popular culture is potential material for their songs.

By Christmas 1988, most of the work on the album was done. In early 1989, the team went to the Record Plant studio to finish the work. It wasn't going to be all work and no play, however. Mike D called a rental shop, and the studio was soon equipped with a large-screen projection television, a Ping-Pong table, a foosball table, an air hockey table, and three pinball machines.

The band did work hard, but there was always somebody playing games, especially Ping-Pong. In fact, at the beginning of the song "3-Minute Rule" you can hear Ping-Pong being played. It was recorded accidentally, and the boys decided to keep it in the song. The games did serve a purpose. They helped everybody unwind from the pressure of getting the album recorded. They were there for another reason, as well. It was a way of getting back at Rick Rubin and their work at Chung King Studio in New York City.

As Mike D said in 1994, as quoted in the book *Paul's Boutique*, "We'd be like going into this bummy studio [while making *Licensed to Ill*] at two in the morning. And then all of a sudden we were here, going into these fancy studios where you pay like $15,000 a day. And we'd just go in there and play Ping-Pong. Seriously."

RECEPTION TO *PAUL'S BOUTIQUE*

Finally, after nearly a year and half of work, the album was released on July 25, 1989. The reviews were amazing. *Time* magazine, in a review by David Hiltbrand, called it, "the most daring, clever record of the year." The *Washington Post* praised the group's artistic growth since *Licensed to Ill*. Everyone expected the album to be another huge hit.

They were wrong. The album reached only number 14 on the *Billboard* charts before quickly sliding back down. The first single, "Hey Ladies," reached number 36 on the *Billboard* 100 and number 10 on the R&B charts. In its first year of release, *Paul's Boutique* sold fewer than one million copies. This was a far cry from the 5 million copies sold of *Licensed to Ill*.

Why was *Paul's Boutique* a commercial failure? There were mistakes made in marketing; the Beastie Boys were not willing to go out on tour to help advertise the album; and they did very few interviews. They wanted to let the music speak for itself.

Unfortunately, publicity is almost always needed to help sell an album, especially one as dense and complicated as

In 1988 the Beastie Boys signed to Capitol Records. They received a two-album deal worth approximately $3 million dollars. Their ties to Def Jam Recordings ended with a barrage of lawsuits and counter-lawsuits. Ultimately, the Beastie Boys and Def Jam agreed to a settlement out of court, and the two parties officially ended their business relationship.

Paul's Boutique. Another problem was that of expectations. Many fans of *Licensed to Ill* wanted to hear more of the same. They wanted to hear songs that sounded like "Fight for Your Right." When they heard the Beastie Boys' new sound, they rejected it.

Both Capitol Records and the Beastie Boys were disappointed in the low sales for *Paul's Boutique,* but they've had the last laugh. *Paul's Boutique* has been recognized as one of the great albums of rock history. *Rolling Stone* magazine named it number 156 on its list of "The 500 Greatest Albums of All Time." *Spin* magazine named it number 12 on its list of "100 Greatest Albums 1985–2005."

Created while they were living in Los Angeles, *Paul's Boutique* can be heard as a homesick love letter from the Beastie Boys to their home city of New York. In its variety, complexity, and artistic integrity, *Paul's Boutique* stands as the pinnacle of their achievements to that date. Stephen Thomas Erlewine wrote the following in All Music:

> The Dust Brothers and Beasties weave a crazy quilt of samples, beats, loops, and tricks ... a romanticized, funhouse reflection of New York where all pop music and culture exists ... a wholly unique record, unlike anything that came before or after ... Musically few hip-hop records have ever been so rich ... Lyrically the Beasties have never been better—not just because their jokes are razor sharp, but because they construct full-bodied narratives and evocative portraits of characters and places.
>
> Few pop records offer this much to savor. And if *Paul's Boutique* only made a modest impact upon its initial release, over time its influence could be heard through pop and rap ... it stands alone as a record of stunning vision, maturity and accomplishment.

With *Paul's Boutique*, the Beastie Boys made a classic. As Rob Sheffield said in the February 6, 2003, *Rolling Stone*, it's "a celebration of American junk culture that is still blowing minds today—even fourteen years of obsessive listening can't exhaust all the musical and lyrical jokes crammed into *Paul's Boutique*."

Despite the lawsuits, the pressures, and their own funloving ways, the Beastie Boys came through with a masterpiece.

Although some critics and many fans initially dismissed the album, *Paul's Boutique* showed the world that they were more than just three "jerks." They were serious musicians who loved doing what they were doing. As MCA said in *Beastie Boys . . . In Their Own Words*, "I would say that if [*Paul's Boutique*] is saying anything, it's saying that we love music. That is, indeed, the central statement in my eyes."

Check Your Head/Ill Communication

After the critical success and commercial failure of *Paul's Boutique*, the boys decided to live in California permanently. They liked the lifestyle that Los Angeles gave them. It also allowed them a lot of ways to stay busy. Mike D busied himself with the formation of the Beastie Boys' new recording label, Grand Royal. Ad-Rock started playing bass with the hardcore band D.F.L. He married Ione Skye in 1991. He also continued to act on occasion, appearing in the movie *Roadside Prophets* in 1992. MCA was beginning his own spiritual journey, one that eventually led him to Buddhism and political activism.

Despite their outside interests, to Mike D, MCA, and Ad-Rock, being the Beastie Boys remained their primary

Following *Paul's Boutique* and before they reunited to make *Check Your Head*, the three members of the Beastie Boys undertook separate ventures. Ad-Rock got married and did some acting. MCA became spiritually and politically active, and Mike D *(above)* proved himself a savvy businessman, initiating ventures such as the recording label Grand Royal and investing in the popular clothing label X-Large.

interest. They began to think about making another record. Ironically, the lack of popular success for *Paul's Boutique* liberated them even more as artists. Expectations for them were lower, so they felt free to explore new ways of making music. They felt they had nothing to lose.

The boys had been spending their time listening to a lot of funk music. Classic 1970s groups like the Meters, Sly and the Family Stone, and the Crusaders were among their favorites.

Funk, they decided, was a direction they wanted to explore. They also decided that, for the first time in years, they wanted to get back to playing instruments.

At first, they started playing in Ad-Rock's apartment. But after neighbors started complaining about hearing music at two in the morning, they realized they would have to move. They decided to build their own recording studio in a space that had been an old ballroom. They called it G-Son in homage to the rental house they used while making *Paul's Boutique,* G Spot. Along with recording equipment, the studio had a few extras only the Beastie Boys would think of. There were video games and a basketball court. There was even a skateboard ramp. (MCA is an avid skateboarder, as well as skier and snowboarder.)

CHECK YOUR HEAD

On the new album, the B-Boys wanted to use less sampling and more of their own music. Over the next year, the boys got together at the studio and played long jam sessions. Jazz, reggae, hardcore: They'd play any style they could think of, and they planned on using all these styles on the new album. Lyrically, though, they were struggling. They thought that a change of location might help them overcome their writer's block, so they went to San Francisco.

When in San Francisco, they received some terrible news. They learned that Dave Scilken, former band member of Adam Horovitz in the Young and the Useless, had died of a drug overdose. Scilken was an old friend of everyone in the band. The boys were devastated at the news of his death, but it inspired them to do their best work.

The album *Check Your Head* was soon finished and released on April 21, 1992. Seventy percent of the tracks were recorded using live instruments. Mike D was on drums, MCA on bass, Ad-Rock on guitar, and Mark "Money Mark" Ramos Nishita on keyboards.

On April 21, 1992, the Beastie Boys released their third album, *Check Your Head*. The album featured the hit songs "So What'cha Want" and "Pass the Mic." The album was more of a return to their punk rock roots, and it received critical and public acclaim.

There was great uncertainty about how the album would be received. Music had changed a great deal since the release of *Paul's Boutique*. Rap had become more hardcore. Alternative rock groups like R.E.M., Nirvana, and Sonic Youth were attracting large audiences. Would the Beastie Boys be able to fit into the new musical landscape?

There was no need to worry. The album was embraced by both critics and the public. The song "Pass the Mic" became a hit in dance clubs. The first official single, "So What'cha Want" became a hit as well. The album went double platinum, peaking at number 10 on the *Billboard* 200. The boys were definitely back.

Their music was getting played on both rap and alternative rock stations. The Beastie Boys were pulling together a whole new audience. Punks, skateboarders, and hip-hop fans were unified in their appreciation of the boys' music. Critics, too, hailed the new album. They appreciated the way the B-Boys had continued to grow as a band. No longer dependent on hip-hop, they used it as just one more musical style. "Lighten Up" and "Something's Got to Give" were funk and jazz inspired. "Time for Livin'" was a return to hardcore punk.

As Stephen Thomas Erlewine wrote on All Music, "Rap . . . was no longer the foundation of their music. It was simply the most prominent in a thick pop-culture gumbo where old school rap sat comfortably with soul-jazz, hardcore punk, white-trash metal, arena rock, Bob Dylan, bossa nova, spacey pop, and hard, dirty funk. . . . This is a whirlwind tour through the Beasties' pop-culture obsessions . . . an alt-rock touchstone of the '90s, something that both set trends and predicted them."

Buoyed by the critical and popular success of the album, the group decided to hit the road in the summer of 1992 with their Check Your Head tour. The tour was a huge success. They played with acts as varied as Sonic Youth, Cypress Hill, and Henry Rollins. By appealing to fans of both rap and punk, they brought together a new kind of audience.

BUSINESSMEN

The Beastie Boys were no longer content to let others control their financial destiny. Their experiences with Def Jam had taught them a valuable lesson. They started their own record label, Grand Royal, which released *Check Your Head*.

They signed new groups to the Grand Royal label, including Sean Lennon, Ben Lee, Cibo Matto, At the Drive-In, and Luscious Jackson, who joined the Beastie Boys on tour. The drummer for Luscious Jackson was the boys' old bandmate, Kate Schellenbach. There was more to Grand Royal than just a record label. They also published a magazine, *Grand Royal*. (The group sold Grand Royal records in 2001.)

The first edition of the magazine came out in 1993 and featured a cover story about Bruce Lee, the famous martial artist and actor. The issue had artwork by legendary funk musician George Clinton and featured interviews with basketball star Kareem Abdul-Jabaar and A Tribe Called Quest's MC, Q-Tip. Anything the boys were interested in made it into the magazine. Mike D did most of the work on the magazine. The 1995 issue is legendary for introducing a new word to the vocabulary of most Americans: "mullet."

The B-Boys were at a new height of popularity. They had been regarded as cool for a long time, but now they were arbiters of cool. People looked to them to see what trends in music and pop culture were going to be. The Beastie Boys began to define what cool was. If the Beasties were doing it, it *had* to be cool.

They decided to return to the recording studio in the fall of 1993. Unlike previous times in the studio, the boys knew what they wanted to do. The record came together quickly. As their longtime recording engineer Mario "Mario C" Caldato Jr. remembers in *The Skills to Pay the Bills*, "That record (*Ill Communication*) was made really fast. After we finished the tour, everyone was excited, like, Wow, let's make another record. And the last record (*Check Your Head*) did really good, so we

Luscious Jackson was just one of the groups signed to the Beastie Boys' label Grand Royal. They released three albums, and had one major hit, "Naked Eye," when signed to the label. In 2000, the band officially broke up. From *left to right,* Kate Schellenbach, Gabby Glaser, Jill Cunniff, and Vivian Trimble pose for this 1994 photograph. Schellenbach was an original member of the Beastie Boys.

went into the studio and we did that record in six months. We had a flow. The band was tight."

The Beastie Boys felt more confident in their abilities. *Ill Communication* was designed to compliment what they accomplished on *Check Your Head.* As MCA says in *The Skills to Pay the Bills,* "On *Ill Communication* we just expanded on what we did on *Check Your Head.* More perfecting those styles—like we could play hardcore tighter than that. With the instrumental stuff, too, we felt like we had advanced during touring."

America was ready for a new Beastie Boys album. The album exploded onto the charts on its release on May 23, 1994.

It debuted at number 1 on the *Billboard* Top 200. It peaked at number 2 on the R&B/Hip-Hop album chart. The single, "Sabotage," became a huge hit on modern-rock charts.

THE MULLET

Everyone knows the haircut known as the mullet. It's short in the front and on the top, but long in the back. Some people who wear it are fond of describing it as "business up front, party in the back!" This means that from the front it looks like something you could wear to work, but in the back, it looks like something wilder that you'd wear out at night. It's like having two hairstyles at once.

What many people don't know is that the term "mullet" was originated by the Beastie Boys. The B-Boys used the term in the 1994 song "Mullet Head." Then, issue number 2 of the group's *Grand Royal* magazine examined the mullet phenomenon in great detail. The article "Mulling Over the Mullet" makes the claim that Mike D was the first to use the term "mullet." Other articles included "Ancient History of the Mullet," "I Was a Twentysomething Mullet Head for a Day" (written by Mike D), and "You Too Can Be a Mullethead."

Obviously, the B-Boys meant it all as a joke, but ironically, they were taken seriously. *The Oxford English Dictionary* (OED) is considered to be the most complete and authoritative dictionary in the world. In 2001, it included the word "mullet" in its lexicon. It also cited the 1995 *Grand Royal* magazine article as the first published use of the word. The lyrics to "Mullet Head" were also included in the entry. The OED said that the term "mullet" was "apparently coined, and certainly popularized, by U.S. hip-hop group the Beastie Boys." Who would ever have imagined that the Beastie Boys would be included in *The Oxford English Dictionary*?

Lollapalooza is a music festival organized by Jane's Addiction frontman Perry Ferrell. The tour featured a wide variety of bands, including alternative, rock, and hip-hop artists. In 1994, the Beastie Boys were asked to headline the tour. In the photograph above, Adam Horovitz, Adam Yauch, and Mike Diamond perform on tour.

The video for "Sabotage," directed by Spike Jonze, was a huge hit on MTV. In it, the B-Boys play 1970s TV policemen. Everything from the costumes to the sets to the look of the video itself is perfect. It is widely considered to be one of the funniest and best videos of its time.

TOURING AND BRANCHING OUT

Based on the success of *Ill Communication*, the Beastie Boys were invited to headline the 1994 Lollapalooza tour. Headlining along with them were artists such as the Smashing Pumpkins,

George Clinton and the P-Funk All Stars, Nick Cave and the Bad Seeds, A Tribe Called Quest, and Green Day. It was a veritable who's who of alternative music. After Lollapalooza ended, the Beastie Boys continued to tour on their own. The tour was called the Quadraphonic Joystick Action tour. The group was so popular that, when tickets for the tour went on sale, they sold out within minutes.

In 1995, the boys also released the little-known EP *Aglio e Olio*. A return to their hardcore roots, the EP has 11 songs and lasts only 11 minutes! It includes such songs as "Believe Me" and "I Want Some." Both of these songs are included on the Beasties' compilation, *The Sounds of Science*.

Throughout the mid-1990s, the Beastie Boys became more and more involved in working for charitable causes, particularly the Milarepa Fund. The royalties for two songs on *Ill Communication*, "Bodhisattva Vow" and "Shambala," were donated to the Milarepa Fund. They played concerts in Los Angeles, New York, and Washington, D.C., with all money going to the Milarepa Fund. In addition, one dollar of every ticket sold for the Quadraphonic Joystick Action tour went to the Milarepa Fund.

What is the Milarepa Fund? How did the Beastie Boys get involved with it? It all goes back to a trip that MCA took to Tibet.

Maturity

Tibet, a country in Asia, is wedged between the People's Republic of China, Burma, Bhutan, Nepal, and India. It is located on the Tibetan Plateau, the world's highest region. Most of the Himalaya Mountains lie within Tibetan borders.

After the release of *Paul's Boutique*, MCA needed to get away for a time. An avid snowboarder, he decided to go to Tibet. There, he met a young activist named Erin Potts. Through her, he became acquainted with modern Tibetan history. What he learned surprised and shocked him.

For centuries, Tibet had been a relatively independent country. Predominantly Buddhist, it was ruled by the Dalai Lama. Chinese armies invaded the peaceful nation in the 1950s because the Chinese government felt that Tibet was

TENZIN GYATSO, 14TH DALAI LAMA

The Dalai Lama is the supreme head of Tibetan Buddhism, similar to the pope's role in Catholicism. The line of Dalai Lamas can be traced back to 1391. When the Dalai Lama dies, it is believed that his soul is reborn or "reincarnated" into that of a new baby; monks search throughout the country, looking for the small child believed to be his reincarnation. When the baby is found and tested, he is brought back to the Tibetan capital of Lhasa to be trained.

The current Dalai Lama, Tenzin Gyatso, is the 14th. He was born in the Tibetan province of Amdo on July 6, 1935. The fifth of 16 children, he was proclaimed the rebirth of the 13th Dalai Lama at the age of five. As part of his test, young Tenzin was shown a group of articles. Some had belonged to the 13th Dalai Lama, some had not. Tenzin correctly identified all of the articles that had belonged to the previous Dalai Lama, stating, "It's mine! It's mine!"

At the age of 15, the new Dalai Lama was also enthroned as the political leader of Tibet. In October of that year, armies of the People's Republic of China entered Tibetan territory. Efforts to reach agreement with the government of China failed, and on March 17, 1959, the Dalai Lama fled Tibet. He arrived in India on March 31 and has lived in exile from his homeland ever since.

While living in exile, the Dalai Lama has tirelessly traveled the world, spreading Buddhism and speaking out about the cause of a free Tibet. In 1989, he was awarded the Nobel Peace Prize for his efforts in the struggle for a liberated Tibet and for his goal to reach a peaceful resolution instead of using violence.

The Dalai Lama is one of today's most beloved public figures. His smiling face, peaceful demeanor, and air of calmness and serenity have made him the public face of Buddhism throughout the world.

historically part of China and it wanted to reassert its authority over the country.

In 1959, the Dalai Lama fled Tibet and began living in exile, out of the country. Under Chinese rule, Tibetan citizens have lost many of their freedoms. They are not allowed to practice their religion as they see fit. Many historic temples have been destroyed. Many Buddhist monks and nuns have been killed.

After learning this, MCA and, through him, the rest of the group, became committed to doing all they could to help free Tibet from Chinese rule. They have worked hard to educate their audiences about the injustices taking place in Tibet.

Together, MCA and Erin Potts founded the Milarepa Fund. They took the name "Milarepa" from an 11th-century Tibetan saint revered for using music to help enlighten people.

The Milarepa Fund was originally started to help distribute the royalties from the songs "Bodhisattva Vow" and "Shambala." It was only fair that the money from those songs should go toward Tibetan freedom. After all, the chants of Tibetan monks had been sampled on both of those songs.

For the Beastie Boys, that was only a beginning. They wanted to do more to help the Tibetan people. To help raise money and public awareness, they started the Tibetan Freedom Concerts. The first concert took place on June 15 and 16, 1996, at the Polo Grounds in San Francisco's Golden Gate Park. More than 100,000 people turned out for the event, making it the largest benefit concert since 1985's Live Aid.

Performers for the first concert included alternative rockers Smashing Pumpkins and Rage Against the Machine; rap groups De La Soul and A Tribe Called Quest; and blues artists Buddy Guy and John Lee Hooker. The list of speakers at the event included former Tibetan prisoners, political activists, and educators. Everyone was happy to get involved for such a worthy cause.

The concert raised over $800,000 for Tibetan causes. It was so successful that the concerts were held annually until 2001.

Adam Yauch speaks at a press conference prior to a 1998 Tibeten Freedom concert in Washington, D.C. The Beastie Boys started the Tibetan Freedom concerts in 1996 in order to raise money and awareness for the Tibetan people. The concerts were held annually until 2001.

These concerts helped to educate the public, especially young people, about the plight of the Tibetan people and helped spur the growth of the worldwide movement Students for a Free Tibet.

Their political involvement with the free Tibet movement affected the Beastie Boys personally as well. MCA became a practicing Buddhist, and the others have incorporated elements of Buddhism into their daily lives. Buddhism helped to bring peace and serenity to all of their lives.

MORE MUSIC

The year 1996 saw the release of the album *The In Sound from Way Out!* A purely instrumental album with no lyrics, it consists of songs recorded between 1992 and 1996. All Music's Stephen Thomas Erlewine writes, "The Beasties have a flair for loose, gritty funk and soul-jazz, and the stuttering, greasy keyboards of Money Mark give the music an extra edge—he helps make the music sound as authentic as anything from the early '70s . . . endlessly enjoyable."

In 1997, the Beastie Boys returned to New York City for the first time in 10 years to make a new record. There, they set up shop in a downtown studio known as the Dungeon. Working with a new DJ, Mix Master Mike, they set to work. The new album was to be called *Hello Nasty*.

On *Hello Nasty*, they combined the sampling of *Paul's Boutique* with the funk and hip-hop of *Check Your Head* and *Ill Communication*. They also added some new styles of music, including old-school soul, electronic beeps and sound effects, Brazilian, and even easy listening. Their rapping remained the same, however: old school, three guys trading off rhymes. This combination of old and new gave *Hello Nasty* an exciting sound.

The album was released on July 14, 1998. In its first week of release, it sold nearly 700,000 copies in the United States alone. It quickly went to number 1 on the U.S. charts, as well as in the

Due to his involvement with the Tibetan freedom movement, Adam Yauch became a practicing Buddhist. Adam Horovitz and Mike D also incorporated Buddhist practices into their daily lives. In the photograph above, The Beastie Boys perform during the 1998 Tibetan Freedom concert in Washington, D.C.

United Kingdom, Germany, Australia, Holland, New Zealand, and Sweden.

The critics, as usual, raved. Stephen Thomas Erlewine of All Music wrote, "*Hello Nasty* is a head-spinning listen loaded with analog synthesizers, old drum machines, call-and-response vocals, freestyle rhyming, futuristic sound effects, and virtuoso turntable scratching . . . what makes it remarkable is how it looks to the future by looking to the past." *Rolling Stone* applauded the album's ambition and musical density in its review: "Hip-hop hasn't unleashed anything this fantastically dense since the heyday of De La Soul and Public Enemy."

Along with rave reviews and renewed popularity, the group began to receive numerous awards for their work. At the 1998 MTV Video Awards, they were awarded the highly coveted Video Vanguard Award for their contribution to music videos. The group is legendary for their innovative, cutting-edge videos, many of which were directed by MCA, using the pseudonym Nathaniel Hornblower. Along with the Video Vanguard Award, they also received the award for Best Hip-Hop Video for "Intergalactic."

The Beastie Boys also received the applause of their peers. They won two Grammy Awards in 1999: the award for Best Alternative Music Album for *Hello Nasty* and the award for Best Rap Performance by a Duo or Group for the "electro-stomp" single "Intergalactic." They were the first group to win Grammys in both the rap and alternative music categories. By winning those awards they proved how well they bridged both musical worlds.

After a long, highly successful tour supporting *Hello Nasty*, the group decided to take a break from recording. This didn't mean, though, that the boys weren't busy.

SIDE VENTURES

MCA oversaw a DVD compilation of their videos, released by Criterion. The band also issued a two-CD compilation of all phases of their career, called *The Sounds of Science*. It came with a book of photographs and liner notes written by the boys themselves, explaining the origins of each of the songs.

They also became increasingly involved in politics. Mike D became involved in the Save Our Environment program. Ad-Rock spoke out on women's rights at the 1999 MTV Video Awards. MCA continued his involvement with the Milarepa Fund. And always, a part of the proceeds from all of their concerts was donated to local charities.

When it was released in 1998, *Hello Nasty* became number one on U.S. charts and received rave reviews from critics and fans alike. They received the Best Hip-Hop Video Music Award, an MTV Video Vanguard Award, and two Grammy Awards. Pictured above, the CD cover for *Hello Nasty*.

A tour was planned for 2000 with the group Rage Against the Machine, but the boys were forced to cancel their involvement when Mike D needed shoulder surgery following a bicycle accident. By the time he had recovered, Rage Against the Machine had disbanded.

The boys were content to let things remain as they were. Their political causes kept them busy and involved. Their personal lives kept them happy. (After divorcing Ione Skye, Ad-Rock married Kathleen Hanna of the bands Bikini Kill and Le Tigre; MCA married Tibetan Dechen Wangdu in a mixed Jewish/Buddhist wedding ceremony; and Mike D married director Tamra Davis, with whom he has had two children, Skyler and Davis.) There were no immediate plans to return to the recording studio. As much as possible, they were living the lives of normal people. As Mike D says in *The Skills to Pay the Bills*, "Mostly our actual lives are incredibly boring and disappointing." For example, during the years following *Hello Nasty*, Ad-Rock spent a lot of time mastering the board game Scrabble!

Things, though, were about to change. The events of September 11, 2001, and its aftermath, gave the Beastie Boys something new to rap about.

Elder Statesmen

The attacks on the World Trade Center and the Pentagon on September 11, 2001, affected every American. As New Yorkers, Adam Yauch, Adam Horovitz, and Mike Diamond were especially distressed by the damage done to their native city. Previously they'd used their celebrity to speak about the wrongs occurring in Tibet. Now, they began to speak out to help their fellow New Yorkers.

On October 28 and 29, just weeks after the 9/11 attacks, the boys headlined the New Yorkers Against Violence benefit concerts. Appearing with other New York artists such as the Strokes and Mos Def, the concerts raised money to help those affected by the attacks. The money was given to the New York Women's Foundation Disaster Relief Fund and to the New York Association for New Americans.

In 2002, to show their support for New York City, the boys started building a new studio facility, Oscilloscope, in downtown Manhattan. It was there that they began work on their first studio album in six years. For the first time in their career, they produced the album themselves. They hoped to give something back to the city and the people they loved. Music, they felt, would bring together and help heal people better then anything else they could do.

The boys interrupted work on the album to record and release a new protest song in March 2003. The song was called "In a World Gone Mad." In it, the boys attacked President George W. Bush and his plans for war in Iraq. The song was available for free download on numerous sites, including the Milarepa Web site, the MTV Web site, MoveOn.org, and Win Without War. The song became the most downloaded track during April 2003.

On April 28, 2004, the first single from their new album debuted. Called "Ch-Check It Out," it played on "The Vegas" episode of the popular television show *The OC*. The new album, *To the 5 Boroughs*, was released on June 15, 2005. The album is a love letter to New York City; its lyrics reflect the boys' love for the city and the ability of its citizens to survive even the worst of calamities. For example, in the song "An Open Letter to NYC" they say, "Brownstones, water towers, trees, skyscrapers / Writers, prize fighters and Wall Street traders / We come together on the subway cars / Diversity unified, whoever you are / We're doing fine on the 1 and 9 line." They also look back at the musical scene that shaped them—the break-dancers, MCs, and DJs. *To the 5 Boroughs* reminded people of the power of music to heal. It made people want to get up and dance again.

It had been six years since the release of *Hello Nasty*, and Beastie Boys fans were eager for a new album. *To the 5 Boroughs* debuted at number 1 on the *Billboard* charts, selling close to 400,000 copies in its first week alone. It also reached number 1 in the United Kingdom, number 2 in Australia, and number 3

The Beastie Boys performed at the New Yorkers Against Violence Concert just weeks after the 9/11 attacks. Since all three members of the group are native New Yorkers, they were very much affected by the World Trade Center tragedy. All proceeds from the concert went to victims of the terrorist attacks. Above, Mike D and Ad-Rock hit the stage.

The Beastie Boys' sixth album, *To the 5 Boroughs*, was a tribute to their hometown of New York. The album not only achieved critical and public acclaim, it also spurred some controversy, with lyrics criticizing President Bush and his presidency. In the photograph above, the Beastie Boys tape an MTV special "Live to the 5 Boroughs" in support of their album.

in Germany in its debut week. It was apparent that even after a six-year absence, the world still wanted to hear what the Beastie Boys were doing.

Critics, too, loved the new album. *Rolling Stone* said "*To the 5 Boroughs* is an exciting, astonishing balancing act: fast, funny and sobering." The magazine gave it a five stars out of five rating. Popmatters raved, "It's their best album since *Paul's Boutique*."

All Music Guide said, "It's rather impressive that they're maturing gracefully, turning into expert craftsmen who can deliver a satisfying listen like this." And the *Onion's* AV Club summed it up nicely, saying, "With *To the 5 Boroughs*, Beastie Boys discover a musical entry way to an earlier, more innocent era, affording listeners the exuberance of youth together with the hard-won wisdom that can only come with experience."

The album was not without controversy. Some people felt that the group's attacks on President Bush and his policies were out of line. Additional controversy erupted when allegations were made that the CD installed spyware when it was inserted

BUDDHISM

Buddhism is one of the world's great religions. It's also known as Buddha Dharma, meaning "the teachings of the awakened one." Buddhism is based on the teachings of Gautama Buddha. He lived on the Indian subcontinent in or around the fifth century B.C. In the centuries following his death, Buddhism spread throughout Asia. Today, it is increasingly practiced in the Western world as well. Buddhism is now thought to be the world's fourth-largest organized religion. The number of adherents is believed to be approximately 350 million worldwide.

The basic tenets of Buddhism are that nothing is fixed or permanent, actions have consequences, and change is possible. Although there are different forms of Buddhism, they share several aspects: a belief in nonviolence, a tolerance of differences, and usually, the practice of meditation. The Buddhist believes that through meditating (which usually means sitting quietly and looking into one's self), anyone can achieve inner peace and happiness.

into the CD drive of a computer. The group denied the allegations, stating that there was no copy protection software on the album sold in the United States and United Kingdom.

NO TIME TO REST

In 2005, Capitol Records released a single disc of the Beastie Boys' greatest hits called *Solid Gold Hits*. Unlike the two-disc compilation *The Sounds of Science*, this CD contained only their biggest hits. It, too, was highly successful. The greatest-hits CD was followed up by their first concert film, *Awesome, I Shot That*. The film captures a live performance on October 9, 2004, at Madison Square Garden. The movie was directed by Adam Yauch under the alias "Nathanial Hornblower." Unlike most concert films though, the movie didn't use professional cameramen. Instead, it was made by the fans themselves.

Fifty fans at the concert were given either DV or High-8 video cameras. They were instructed to keep their cameras rolling at all times. The footage was then edited into a movie. The movie was first screened in January 2006 to an audience of the same fans who shot the movie. It was given a general release on March 31, 2006. *Esquire* magazine praised the film: "stunning footage and imaginative storytelling showcase unforgettable music." *Film Threat* said that the movie "reinvents the concert film like no other before it." Once again, the Beastie Boys had taken a recognized genre, the concert film, and made it their own.

The Beastie Boys now stood as the elder statesmen of hip-hop. Few if any hip-hop groups have had as long or as successful a career. Not content to rest on their laurels, in the summer of 2006, the boys announced that they were writing songs for a new album. The album, called *The Mix-Up*, is their first full album of entirely new and original instrumental material. It was released in June 2007.

In a career that has spanned more then 20 years, the Beastie Boys have influenced both hip-hop and rock history, and in their

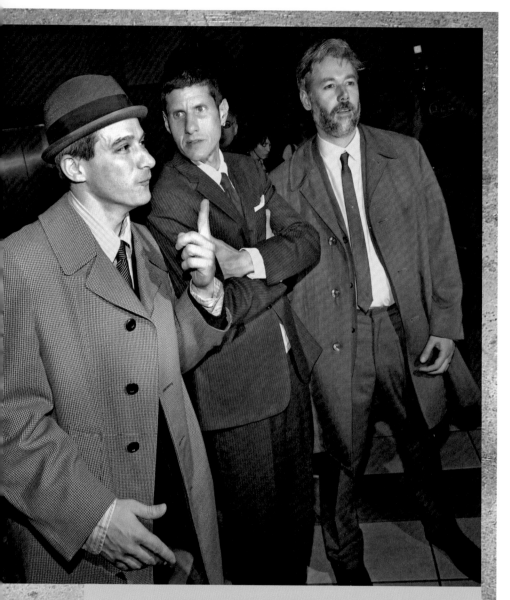

In the photograph above, The Beastie Boys attend the premiere of their film *Awesome, I Shot That*. The film features a live Beastie Boys performance, which was shot by 50 fans in attendance. Adam Yauch, the director of the movie, edited the footage taken from all the fans and created a unique concert film.

innovative blending of rap and punk, they have inspired nearly every band that has come after them. Groups such as Korn and Limp Bizkit would not exist without the Beastie Boys.

Their use of sampling techniques has been equally influential. Artists like Beck are deeply in their debt. They've even set fashion trends, mixing skater and hip-hop urban wear in a style that some call Skaballer.

However, the Beastie Boys are not just a group—they are three strong individuals. Each of them brings something different to the group, and that is what has helped them to survive for so long. That is what has helped to make them great.

As Mix Master Mike says in *The Skills to Pay the Bills*, "What makes them special is that their personalities are so different. Adam [Horovitz] is the vehicle, the conductor—he comes in with a big bag of beats, and we all kind of follow that, on top. Yauch, it's his voice, his delivery, his vocals. He takes his writing very seriously, puts a lot of thought into it. But he's like the wild card. And Mike D is the b-boy. He brings the b-boy element."

What's truly remarkable is that after all this time, the boys are still best friends. Many groups start out as best friends but grow apart due to the pressures of success. Not the Beastie Boys. Even a quarter century after the release of their first EP, *Polly Wog Stew*, they still enjoy recording and hanging out together. As Mike D says in *The Skills to Pay the Bills*, "At the end of the day, we're doing this for ourselves, to make ourselves happy. And that hasn't changed in all these years. That was the game plan from day one."

DISCOGRAPHY

1982 *Polly Wog Stew* (EP)
1986 *Licensed to Ill*
1989 *Paul's Boutique*
1993 *Check Your Head*
1994 *Ill Communication*
1995 *Aglio e Olio* (EP)
1996 *The In Sound from Way Out!*
1998 *Hello Nasty*
1999 *The Sounds of Science*
2004 *To the 5 Boroughs*
2005 *Solid Gold Hits*
2007 *The Mix-Up*

1964   Adam Yauch is born on August 5 in Brooklyn, New York.

1965   Michael Diamond is born on November 20 in New York City.

1966   Adam Horovitz is born on October 31 in South Orange, New Jersey.

1981   The earliest lineup of the Beastie Boys—Michael Diamond, Adam Yauch, Kate Schellenbach, and John Berry—play their first show at Yauch's 17th birthday party. They are immediately signed to a record deal.

1982   Their first EP, *Polly Wog Stew*, is released.

1983   John Berry leaves the band and is replaced by Adam Horovitz of the Young and the Useless. Kate Schellenbach also leaves. The new group records "Cooky Puss," their first hip-hop recording.

1984   "Rock Hard/Beastie Groove" is released.

1986   The group's first album, *Licensed to Ill*, is released. It becomes the first rap album to reach number one on the pop charts. The single "(You Gotta) Fight for Your Right (to Party)" becomes a huge hit on radio and MTV.

1989   Their second album, *Paul's Boutique*, is released to critical acclaim and disappointing sales.

1992   *Check Your Head* is released. With live instruments and a fresh sound, it is a major hit.

1993   Grand Royal, the group's record label, is founded. It is followed with ventures into magazine publishing and fashion.

1994   *Ill Communication*, the group's fourth album, is released. It enters the charts at number one.

1995   After a major sold-out concert tour, the band releases the hardcore EP *Aglio e Olio.*

1996   The first Tibetan Freedom Concert is held in San Francisco's Golden Gate Park. Over 100,000 attendees come to hear great music and to learn about the plight of the Tibetan people. The funk instrumental album *The In Sound from Way Out!* is released.

1998   *Hello Nasty,* the group's fifth album, is released. It is a huge popular and critical success.

2001   Following the terror attacks of September 11, the group organizes the New Yorkers Against Violence benefit.

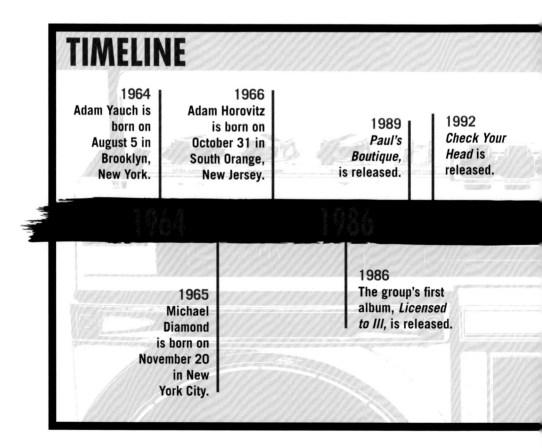

TIMELINE

1964
Adam Yauch is born on August 5 in Brooklyn, New York.

1966
Adam Horovitz is born on October 31 in South Orange, New Jersey.

1989
Paul's Boutique, is released.

1992
Check Your Head is released.

1964   1986

1965
Michael Diamond is born on November 20 in New York City.

1986
The group's first album, *Licensed to Ill,* is released.

2004 The Beastie Boys record and release their first self-produced album, *To the 5 Boroughs.*

2006 Release of the documentary film *Awesome, I Shot That!*

2007 The Beastie Boys release *The Mix-Up,* their first album of original instrumental material.

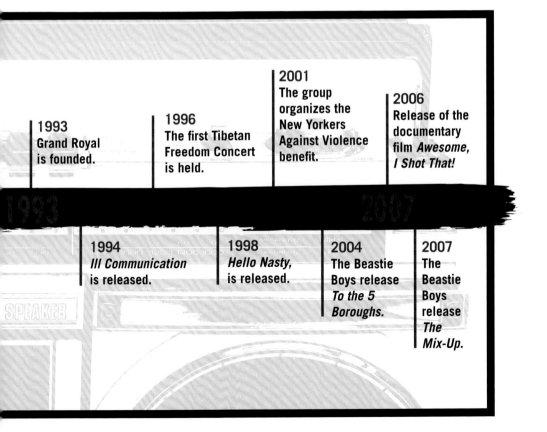

1993
Grand Royal is founded.

1996
The first Tibetan Freedom Concert is held.

2001
The group organizes the New Yorkers Against Violence benefit.

2006
Release of the documentary film *Awesome, I Shot That!*

1994
Ill Communication is released.

1998
Hello Nasty, is released.

2004
The Beastie Boys release *To the 5 Boroughs.*

2007
The Beastie Boys release *The Mix-Up.*

▶ ▶▶ GLOSSARY ■ ❚❚

DJ   Short for "disc jockey." In hip-hop, the DJ handles the turntables, creating the backing music.

EP   Short for "extended play." It is a record that contains more than one song (unlike a single), but with fewer songs than a full-length album.

exile   Someone, who, either by choice or force, lives away from his or her home and country.

hardcore   An intense version of punk rock featuring short, loud, and often angry songs with exceptionally fast tempos and chord changes.

hip-hop   A form of music that sprang up in urban, largely African-American communities. It rarely uses live instruments, but instead is based on prerecorded instruments and a steady stream of break beats, usually accompanied by rhythmic rhyming verse, known as rapping.

MC   Originally short for "master of ceremonies." In hip-hop, the MC puts down the rhymes over the back beats and music.

record label   A record label is a brand name created by companies that specialize in manufacturing, distributing, and promoting both audio and video recordings. The name derives from the paper label at the center of phonograph records (which have now been replaced by CDs).

sample   A small part of a recorded song that is used as part of the music for a new recorded song.

BIBLIOGRAPHY

Diehl, Matt. "Ill Communication," *Rolling Stone*. Available online. http://www.rollingstone.com/reviews/album/253086/ill-communication.

Erlewine, Stephen Thomas. "Beastie Boys Biography," All Music. Available online. http://www.allclassical.com/cg/amg.dll.

———. "Check Your Head," All Music. Available online. http://allclassical.com/cg/amg.dll?p=amg&sql=10:8x5tk6dx9brf.

———. "Hello Nasty," All Music. Available online. http://www.allclassical.com/cg/amg.dll?p=amg&sql-10:d9u1z83a1yv8.

———. "Ill Communication," All Music. Available online. http://www.allclassical.com/cg/amg.dll?p=amg&sql=10:tvge4j371wal.

———. "Licensed to Ill," All Muisc. Available online. http://allclassical.com/cg/amg.dll?p=amg&sql=10:699yxdsbjolk.

———. "Paul's Boutique," All Music. Available online. http://allclassical.com/cg/amg.dll?0=amg&sq=10:yeabpj6bojsa.

Forget, Thomas. *The Beastie Boy*. New York: Rosen Publishing Group, 2006.

Handelman, David. "Rude Boys," *Rolling Stone*. Available online. http://ww.rollingstone.com/news/story/6222767/rude_boys.

Heatley, Michael. *Beastie Boys…In Their Own Words*. London: Omnibus Press, 1999.

LeRoy, Dan. *Paul's Boutique*. New York: The Continuum International Publishing Group Inc., 2006.

"Licensed to Ill," *Rolling Stone*. Available online. http://www.rollingstone.com/news.story/6599146/127_licensed_to_ill.

Light, Alan. *The Skills to Pay the Bills: The Story of the Beastie Boys.* New York: Three Rivers Press, 2005.

O'Mahony, Liam. "Beastie Boys Get Better With Age," 14850 online. Available online. http://www.14850.com/magazine/9507/music.html.

Sheffield, Rob. "Paul's Boutique," *Rolling Stone.* Available online. http://www.rollingstone.com/reviews/album/117996/pauls_boutique.

Touré. "Hello Nasty," *Rolling Stone.* Available online. http://www.rollingstone.com/reviews/album/111416/hello_nasty.

Young, Jayson. "Licensed to Ill," Rap Reviews. Available online. http://www.rapreviews.com/archive/BTTL_licensed.html.

▸ ➤ FURTHER READING ▪ ⏸

BOOKS

Green, Jared. *Examining Pop Culture: Rap and Hip-Hop.* Farmington Hills, Mich.: Greenhaven Press, 2002.

Levy, Patricia. *Tibet* (Cultures of the World). New York: Benchmark Books, 1999.

Light, Alan. *The Vibe History of Hip Hop.* New York: Three Rivers Press, 1999.

Masar, Brendon. *The History of Punk Music.* San Diego: Lucent Books, 2006.

Wilkinson, Philip, and Peggy Morgan. *Buddhism* (Eyewitness Books). New York: DK Children, 2003.

WEB SITES

www.beastieboys.com

www.beastieboysannotated.com

www.freetibet.org

www.inkblotmagazine.com/beastie_mothership.htm

www.milarepa.org

www.studentsforafreetibet.org

▸ ▸ PHOTO CREDITS ▪ ‖

PAGE

▸ ▸▸ ABOUT THE AUTHORS ▪ ‖

DENNIS ABRAMS is the author of several books for Chelsea House, including biographies of Barbara Park, Anthony Horowitz, Ty Cobb, Hamid Karzai, and Eminem. He attended Antioch College, where he majored in English and communications. A voracious reader since the age of three, Dennis currently lives in Houston with his partner of 18 years, two dogs, and three cats.

CHUCK D redefined rap music and hip-hop culture as leader and cofounder of legendary rap group Public Enemy. His messages addressed weighty issues about race, rage, and inequality with a jolting combination of intelligence and eloquence. A musician, writer, radio host, television guest, college lecturer, and activist, he is the creator of Rapstation.com, a multiformat home on the Web for the vast global hip-hop community.